Table of contents

FOREWORD 7

LEVEL 1: FOUNDATIONS 10

THE FACTS 10
    Spain 11
    Latin America 17
YOUR FIRST TEXT IN SPANISH 21
PRONUNCIATION 22
    Alphabet 22
    Pronunciation rules 23
    Vowels 25
    Consonants 26
GRAMMAR 27
    Articles 27
    Subject pronouns 27
    Possessive pronouns 28
    Interrogative pronouns 28
    Tenses 29
    Verbs „ser/estar" 30
    Verbs „haber/tener" 33
    Other modal verbs 35
    Verbs „traer/llevar" 36
    Verbs „ir/venir" 38
    Conjugations -ar,-er,-ir 39
    Reflexive Verbs 41
    Negation 43
VOCABULARY 44
    Top 20 44
    The numbers 45
    Days of the week 46
    The months 47
    The seasons 47
    The colours 48
    The time 48
EXERCISES & GAMES – EJERCICIOS Y JUEGOS 49

LEVEL 2: THE ARRIVAL 52

AT THE AIRPORT – EN EL AEROPUERTO 52
   Top phrases 52
   At the check-in counter 52
   At the customs 53
   Baggage 53
   On the plane 53
MEANS OF TRANSPORTATION – MEDIOS DE TRANSPORTE 54
   Bus 54
   Train 54
   Taxi 55
   Car 55
   Tram 57
   Underground/subway 57
   Bike 57
   Boat 58
EXERCISES & GAMES 59

LEVEL 3: ACCOMMODATION 61

TOP PHRASES 61
SEARCHING 61
BOOKING 63
CHECK-IN 63
COMPLAINTS 64
CHECK-OUT 65
CAMPING 65
   BBQ time! 66
HOLIDAY APARTMENT 66
EXERCISES & GAMES 67

LEVEL 4: EATING & DRINKING 69

TOP PHRASES 69
MEALS 69
RESTAURANTS 70
   Orders 71
IN THE BAR 78
AT THE COFFEE SHOP 79
   Kinds of coffee 79
   Kinds of tea 80
   Cakes 80

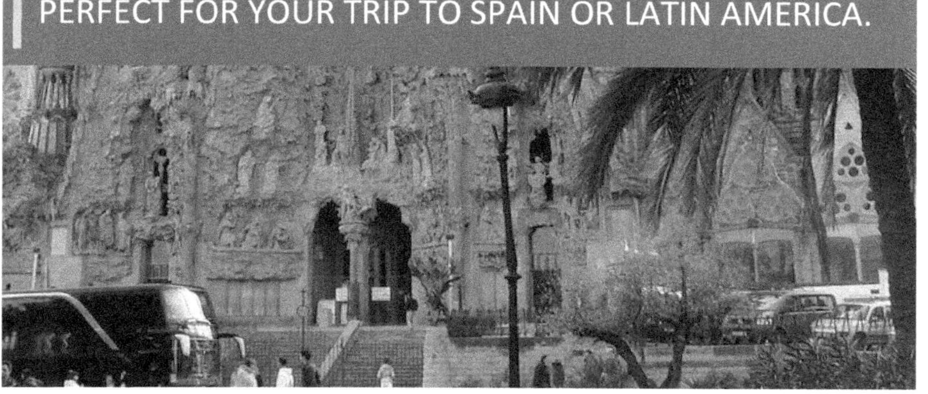

PLD

Learning Spanish for adults made easy... in 2 weeks!

LEO BABEL

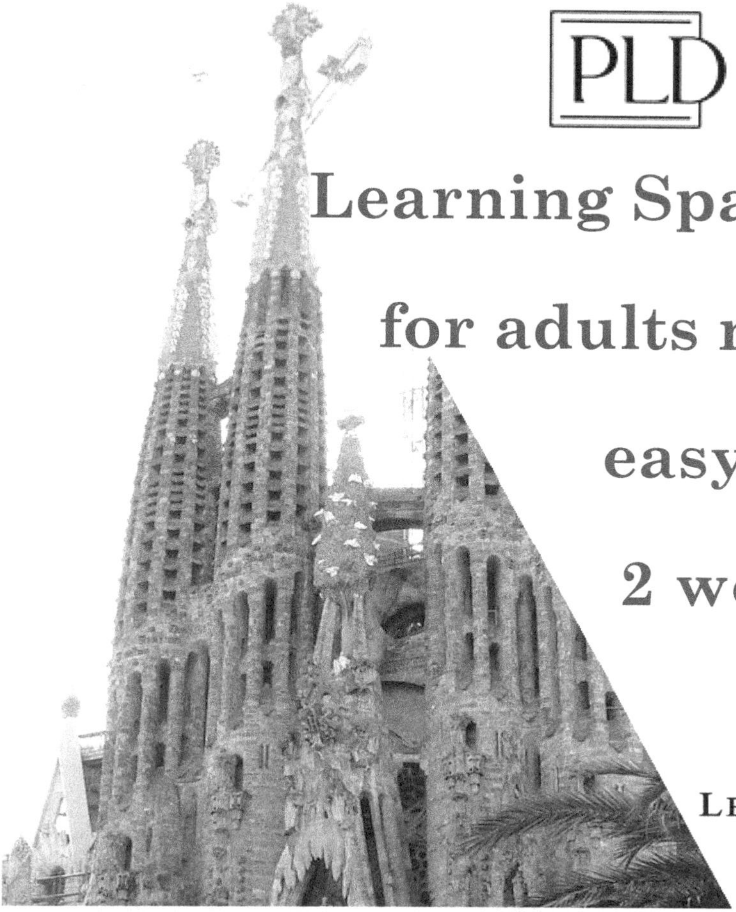

YOUR SPANISH WORKBOOK FOR TRAVEL AND DAILY USE.
LEARN SPANISH HAVING FUN AND WITHOUT EFFORT.
PERFECT FOR YOUR TRIP TO SPAIN OR LATIN AMERICA.

<u>**Disclaimer**</u>
Please note that simply reading a book is not sufficient to learn a language. Active engagement and investment of time and effort are required on the part of the reader to fully understand and apply the concepts presented in the book. It is important to approach the material with an open mind and a willingness to learn and grow.

Learning Spanish for adults made easy… in 2 weeks!
1st edition March 2020
2nd edition April 2023

ISBN: 978-3-949762-25-3

Imprint

PLD Publishing
საქართველო, თბილისი,
ნადიკვარის III ქმჩაქ, N 15

Other drinks 80
EXERCISES & GAMES 81

LEVEL 5: CITY, MOUNTAIN OR BEACH? 82

CITY 82
Top phrases 82
Places of interest 82
Museums & art galleries 84
Tours 85
Travelling with… 85
BEACH OR MOUNTAIN? 87
The weather 87
For mountain lovers 88
For beach lovers 90
EXERCISES & GAMES 92

LEVEL 6: GOING SHOPPING 95

AT THE MALL 95
CLOTHING SHOP 96
BOOKSHOP 97
AT THE CONSUMER ELECTRONICS RETAILER 98
SOUVENIR SHOP 99
AT THE MARKET 100
AT THE FLEA MARKET 100
AT THE SUPERMARKET 101
For meat lovers 101
For veggies 101
For vegans 102
EXERCISES & GAMES 103

LEVEL 7: SPORTS AND EVENTS 106

SPORT 106
Football / Soccer 106
Gym 108
Other sports 109
CONCERTS 110
AT THE CHURCH 110
BULLFIGHTING 111
EXERCISES & GAMES 112

LEVEL 8: IT'S PARTY TIME! 113

Top phrases 113
Meeting new people 113
Flirting 114
   Breaking the ice: pick-up lines 114
   Romantic 115
   Seductive 115
   Refusal 115
   Reciprocal interest 116
   The temperature rises... 116
Exercises & games 116

LEVEL 9: LATIN AMERICAN SPANISH 118

Pronunciation 118
Grammar 120
Vocabulary 121
Exercises & games 123

LEVEL 10: SLANG 124

Slang in Spain 124
Slang in Latin America 125
Exercises & games 127

SOLUTIONS 129

BIBLIOGRAPHY 134

ACKNOWLEDGMENTS 135

LEGAL 136

Foreword

Congratulations! You have made an excellent decision. You have taken action in order to learn one of the most widespread languages in the world.

The main goal of this book is teaching Spanish in a relaxing and funny way, that's why the writing style is casual. I hope you're ok with that.

And what is your goal?

You are planning your next trip to the Canary Islands and would like to be able to order your big pint of beer on the beach in Spanish?

Or possibly a party travel to Ibiza?

Maybe you met a Spaniard/Latino for the first time and you want to impress him/her in their mother tongue?

Or you need some basic Spanish to communicate with the Latinos in your town?

And you want to learn it all in an easy and entertaining way without needing to browse thick and boring textbooks?

Either way, regardless of your motivation, you are in the right place! I am a language lover with the clear vocation of teaching once I have learnt some languages myself. Therefore, I decided to publish language books, this time in English. I have worked on this project passionately, so I hope you can benefit from that by learning a lot.

Maybe you are wondering why I am qualified for this book you're holding or listening to? I speak Spanish as my mother tongue but, apart from that, I also have a good command of five other languages and have other languages learnt at some point and I can express myself. So be confident that you are in good hands.

I want you to learn Spanish quickly and in a funny way, thus the book covers the basics so that you have a good command after... just 2 weeks!

The contents of this book are structured in 10 different chapters (called "levels" here). The first level focuses on the basics, an introduction to the Spanish-speaking countries and what you need to know first. From levels 2 to 8 we describe different situations, e.g. when you arrive at the airport, or we want to order some food or at the mall, among others. Level 9 focuses on the characteristics of South American Spanish and the last level no. 10 goes one step further. Here, you can learn colloquial expressions to sound like a local.

On each level you can find some vocabulary and the most usual phrases from each category, and some games and exercises are suggested at the end of each level so that you test your newly acquired concepts. The solutions to these exercises conclude this textbook.

I suggest this schedule in 14 days, but you can plan it according to your rhythm:

Day 1: Level 1 – The facts-Your first text in Spanish

Day 2: Level 1 – Pronunciation through grammar: „haber/tener"

Day 3: Level 1 – Grammar: Other modal verbs through negation

Day 4: Level 1 – Vocabulary

Day 5: Level 2

Day 6: Level 3

Day 7: Level 4

Day 8: Level 5

Day 9: Level 6

Day 10: Level 7

Day 11: Level 8

Day 12: Level 9

Day 13: Level 10

Day 14: Review everything quietly!

In case you want to learn this language a little bit more deeply and precisely, follow the Advanced tips ▶▶. You don't need these tips at all costs for the learning process, but it will help you if you want to dominate the language more.

To maximize your learning success, you can play all Spanish audio content related to this book as many times as you want to practice your listening comprehension. These audio contents recorded by native speakers are marked in the book with this icon below:

Get used to the perfect pronunciation from day 1! Simply follow this link to download the audio recordings!

https://pld-publishing.com/audio-spa

I look forward to your success and wish you loads of fun while reading. Ready, steady, go!

Leo Babel

Level 1

Foundations

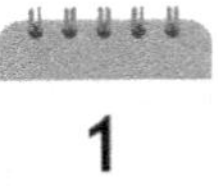

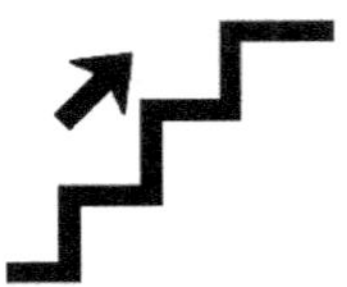

You obviously have to start with the basics, and then you can build on the subsequent levels. Ideally, you work on this level before your trip.

The facts

Spanish is, as you surely already know, one of the most spoken languages in the whole world. *In 2019, about 483 million people have Spanish as mother tongue, most of them in South America, and 7,6% of the world population speaks Spanish[1].*

Spanish is a Romance language that emerged as an evolution of Latin. Other Romance languages are Portuguese, Italian, French or Romanian. All of these languages have certain similarities in vocabulary or grammar, which eases learning any of these once you understand the connections.

Spanish is the official language in Spain, together with Galician (in Galicia), Catalan (in Catalonia, the Valencian Community and the Balearic Islands) and Basque (in Basque Country and Navarra). In Europe, Spanish is often spoken in Andorra and Gibraltar.

The majority of speakers can be found in America. Spanish is the official language in (from north to south): Mexico, Cuba, Dominican Republic, Puerto Rico, Guatemala, El Salvador, Honduras, Nicaragua, Costa Rica, Panama, Colombia, Venezuela, Ecuador, Peru, Bolivia, Chile, Paraguay, Argentina and Uruguay. Spanish is, after English, a very important language in the United States due to the influence of the Latin community, especially in the southern states (California, New Mexico, Arizona, Texas, Florida). In Belize, Spanish is also spoken by a significant number of residents.

Outside of Europe and America, Spanish is also the official language in Equatorial Guinea. Spanish is spoken in the Philippines too, but it is not promoted.

---

[1] EL ESPAÑOL: UNA LENGUA VIVA Informe 2019 - Instituto Cervantes

Since the vast majority of speakers are either in Spain or Latin America, we focus on these regions in this book.

Spain

Spain is located in Southern Europe, south of France. The biggest area is in the Iberian Peninsula. The Canary Islands (in Africa) and the Balearic Islands, east of the mentioned peninsula, along with the autonomous cities Ceuta and Melilla, comprise the country.

The capital city Madrid is in the very center of the peninsula. Other main cities are, among others, Barcelona, Valencia, Sevilla, Granada, Palma de Mallorca or Santa Cruz de Tenerife.

Spain is ranked second for the countries with the most visitors, after France[2]. Spain is popular for the food (the beloved tapas!), its mild weather, its monuments, the beaches and much more. The most famous monuments include:

---

[2]   https://www.20minutos.es/noticia/3779875/0/espana-segundo-pais-mundo-turistas-recibe-millones/

1.	Puerta de Alcalá	Madrid
2.	Sagrada Familia	Barcelona
3.	Parc Güell	Barcelona
4.	La Giralda	Sevilla
5.	Plaza de España	Sevilla
6.	Alhambra	Granada
7.	Catedral	Santiago de Compostela
8.	Alcázar	Toledo
9.	Acueducto	Segovia
10.	Mezquita	Córdoba

Popular festivals in Spain

Spain is also known for its celebrations, some of which are internationally acknowledged. The following ones are definitely worth it:

Tamborrada

When: 20th January

Where: San Sebastián, Basque Country

Description: This drum festival is a 24-hour march through the city. Men wear cook or soldier clothing, women the traditional Basque costume. It is undoubtedly one of the loudest celebrations in Spain.

Carnaval *(Carnival)*

When: February or March

Where: Throughout Spain, the most renowned ones in Tenerife and Cádiz

Description: The Carnival is hugely celebrated in Spain. The most popular Carnival celebrations can be found in the Canary Islands (Tenerife and Gran Canaria), where the Carnival Queen and the Carnival Drag Queen (Las Palmas, Gran Canaria) are announced after an exciting competition; and in Cadiz, also very well known for a song contest which starts several weeks before the carnival. The street parades are very popular and lots of imaginative costumes make the Spanish carnival unforgettable.

Fallas

When: 15th-19th March

Where: Valencia, Valencian Community

Description: The fire festival par excellence. Figures made of wood, cardboard and cork are built for this festival and are exhibited in the streets of Valencia. From March 1st and until March 19th, St. Joseph's Day, very loud fireworks (Mascletà) are lit in the daylight, beautiful colorful fireworks at night. The monuments are burned late on the night of 20th March (Nit de la Cremà). For more information, check my YouTube video *"Valencian Fallas: get to know this World Heritage Festivity"* (Leo Babel Spanish).

Semana Santa *(Holy Week)*

When: March or April

Where: throughout Spain, the most famous processions in Seville, Cordoba, Cáceres, Murcia or Valladolid

Description: The processions in Spain are very popular. In every village and city, you will find brotherhoods belonging to the churches, which march through the city with the images (pasos) of Christ or Mary while singing traditional songs.

Feria de Abril

When: April, 7 days long (always after Easter)

Where: Seville, Andalusia

Description: Colourful tents are set up, people wear the traditional costumes (*traje de flamenco*), flamenco is danced, the horse-drawn carriages ride through the fairground.

Fiesta de los Patios

When: May

Where: Córdoba, Andalusia

Description: The beautiful courtyards (*patios*) are exhibited to the public. Colourful flower pots and the beautiful architecture of the courtyards are particularly worth seeing.

San Isidro

When: May

Where: Madrid

Description: The popular festival in honour of the patron saint San Isidro is celebrated by many on the San Isidro meadow in the Spanish capital. The world's famous bullfights take place within this month in the bullring "Las Ventas".

Romería del Rocío

When: Pentecost

Where: El Rocío (Almonte), Andalusia

Description: The faithful (Catholic) make a pilgrimage to El Rocío and honour the Virgin of El Rocío. The pilgrims wear Andalusian costumes and go to El Rocío on foot or by horse and cart.

San Fermín

When: July

Where: Pamplona, Navarre

Description: This world-renowned feast attracts people from all over the world. The bull runs early in the morning are very popular. Wild bulls are led to the bullring and the animals follow some brave individuals, dressed in white and with a red scarf around their necks, who run in front of them. A huge crowd gathers at the opening event (*chupinazo*) and the closing event (where the "*Pobre de mí*" - "Oh, poor me" - is sung).

La Tomatina

When: Last Wednesday in August

Where: Buñol, Valencia

Description: A crazy tomato battle. Party people throw a ton of tomatoes to each other for pure fun (first crushed so that it doesn't hurt so much!). You can imagine the result: red garbage everywhere in the city, and clothes to be thrown away. In any case it is not recommended for children!

Descenso del Sella *(Sella descent)*

When: early August

Where: Arriondas and Ribadesella, Asturias

Description: A canoe festival where many competitors row a 20 km long course through the Sella river. Cider (Sidra) and local music are definitely included.

Fiestas del Pilar

When: October

Where: Zaragoza, Aragón

Description: This festival is celebrated in honour of the Spanish patron saint, the Virgin of El Pilar. The central event takes place on 12th October (Spanish National Day), when many of the faithful march with their bouquets of flowers towards the Cathedral Square. The flowers are affixed to a high wooden structure. These flowers are collected and these create a colourful dress for the Virgin.

Spain joined the European Union in 1986 and the euro is the currency since 2001.

An interesting fact is that the Spanish national anthem has no recognized lyrics.

Latin America

A large majority of South and Central America speaks Spanish. Because of the wide area, from Mexico to Argentina, there are many different dialects. In any case, Spanish in America has certain characteristics that distinguish it from the language spoken in Spain. More on this in level 9.

Some relevant American cities are México DF (Mexico), La Habana (Cuba), Ciudad de Panamá (Panama), Bogotá (Colombia), Lima (Peru), La Paz (Bolivia), Santiago de Chile (Chile) or Buenos Aires (Argentina).

Latin America is very diverse and culturally rich. Therefore, we have to mention some of its most famous sights:

1.   Machu Picchu   Peru
2.   The Moais   Isla de Pascua (Chile)
3.   Catedral Primada   Colombia
4.   Angel of Independence   Mexico
5.   Obelisk   Buenos Aires
6.   Bolivar Square   Venezuela
7.   Peace Column   Uruguay
8.   Chichen Itzá   Mexico
9.   Tikal   Guatemala
10.   National Flag Memorial   Rosario (Argentina)
11.   Salar de Uyuni   Bolivia
12.   Freedom House   Sucre (Bolivia)

Popular festivals in Latin America

Some Latin American feasts or events are well known, such as:

Día de los Muertos *(Day of the Dead)*

When:	End of October - beginning of November (All Hallows' Day)
Where:	Mexico
Description:	The Mexicans go to the cemetery and visit their deceased, who are honoured in that private colourful altars are set with their favourite foods and drinks. This festival is not melancholic though, but rather entertaining, because the most beautiful anecdotes are remembered.

Festival de Cosquín *(Cosquin Folk Festival)*

When:	January (9 days long)
Where:	Cosquín, Córdoba, Argentina
Description:	Argentina's main folk music festival.

Fiesta nacional del Chamamé *(Chamamé National Festival)*

When:	January
Where:	Corrientes, Argentina
Description:	Chamamé, a genre of folk music from Eastern Argentina, Paraguay, Bolivia, Chile and Uruguay, is sung.

Fiesta Nacional del Choripán *(Choripán National Festival)*

When:	February
Where:	Cordoba, Argentina
Description:	Barbecue party, where the typical 'choripán' (sausage bread) is tasted.

Carnaval de Barranquilla

When:	February/March
Where:	Barranquilla, Colombia
Description:	It is the most important festival in Colombia. The battle of the flowers (*Batalla de flores*) and the street procession (*Gran Parada*) are very popular.

Carnaval de blancos y negros *(Blacks and Whites' Carnival)*

When:	January
Where:	Pasto, Colombia
Description:	The people make up their faces black or white (on Blacks' or Whites' Day, respectively) and the cultural diversity is experienced: African culture, the cultural inheritance from the Spaniards...

Feria de las flores *(Flower fair)*

When:	August
Where:	Medellin, Colombia
Description:	The Silleteros parade (*Silleteros* are huge colourful corollas) is the central event of this festival.

Feria de Manizales

When: January

Where: Manizales, Colombia

Description: Famous for the bullfighting festival, inspired from the Feria de Abril in Seville. Another event is a beauty contest called "International Coffee Queen", where Colombian coffee is advertised.

Festividades de las Ñatitas

When: November

Where: La Paz, Bolivia

Description: The locals preserve the *Ñatitas* (skulls) at home as a protection against illness or spirits. In this festival, they bring the skulls to the church of the main cemetery in La Paz. The *Ñatitas* are blessed; coca or cigarettes donated.

Carnaval de Oruro

When: February

Where: Oruro, Bolivia

Description: The pilgrims walk to the sanctuary from Socavón, where the Virgin of Socavón is located.

An interesting fact is that most South Americans are Catholic.

Your first text in Spanish

Reading exercises are essential for learning a new language. That is why, before we even start with pronunciation or grammar, you will find a text in Spanish in the first place. It is perfectly fine if you do not understand anything or very little. Anyway, you'd be surprised that there are some Spanish words which are similar to English terms (e.g. eliminate – *eliminar*). Understanding other Romance languages, like Italian or French, is definitely beneficial to your learning process.

Begin by reading the text (<u>without</u> audio recordings) and assimilate the first foreign terms -the terms highlighted in bold will be covered in Level 1-.

*„**Son las ocho de la mañana**. El despertador suena y Pedro **quiere** dormir, pero es **lunes** y **debe ir** a **trabajar**. Sin embargo, sabe que las vacaciones de Navidad están ya muy cerca y pronto podrá visitar a su familia. Ahora vive lejos de su gente.*

*Se despierta y ducha antes de tomar un desayuno apetitoso y mira el **reloj**. Es hora de **ir** a la oficina y, al **no tener coche**, debe tomar el transporte público. Puede elegir entre el autobús o el tren, y **hoy** escoge el tren. El tren entra en el andén de la estación y Pedro se sube al tren. Durante el viaje empieza a soñar con esas vacaciones de verano en la playa. Allí reservó **siete** noches en un hotel cerca del mar. Espera poder relajarse y también visitar la ciudad cercana a apenas **veinte** kilómetros. Allí la comida es deliciosa y las fiestas son muy populares. Antes de volver de vuelta a **casa**, **irá** a ver un partido de fútbol de su equipo preferido.*

*Pedro llega a la oficina, pero el día será corto. Después de **trabajar** empezarán ya sus vacaciones de Navidad.”*

Listen to the audio recording for this text and identify which parts you pronounced differently. A good technique to improve your pronunciation is 'shadowing'. Here's how it works: you read out loud while listening to it a few times. You can also repeat after a tiny delay, at your own pace. You have taken a small step forward!

Once you are done with this book, I suggest you come back to this section and read this text again. I am sure that your reading comprehension will have improved!

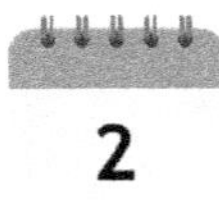

2

Letter (uppercase)	Letter (lowercase)	Pronunciation	Example		ENG
A	a	/a/	amor		*love*
B	b	/b/	bien		*good, well*
C	c	/θ/	cera	(1)	*wax*
		/k/	coche		*car*
D	d	/d/	dar		*give*
E	e	/e/	elemento		*element*
F	f	/f/	fábrica		*factory*
G	g	/g/	gracias	(2)	*thanks*
H	h	//	hola	(3)	*hello*
I	l	/i/	idea		*idea*
J	j	/h/	jamón		*ham*
K	k	/k/	kiosko		*kiosk*
L	l	/l/	lado	(4)	*side*
M	m	/m/	mal		*bad*
N	n	/n/	no		*no*
Ñ	ñ	/ny/	España	(5)	*Spain*
O	o	/ɒ/	ópera		*opera*
P	p	/p/	perro		*dog*
Q	q	/k/	queso	(6)	*cheese*
R	r	/r/	rosa	(7)	*rose*
S	s	/s/	sol	(8)	*sun*
T	t	/t/	terminal		*terminal*
U	u	/ʊ/	uña		*nail*
V	v	/v/	vaca	(9)	*cow*
W	w	/w/	whisky		*whisky*
X	x	/ks/	taxi		*taxi*
Y	y	/j/	yo		*I*
Z	z	/θ/	zapato	(10)	*shoe*

Pronunciation rules

(Indication: the constructions between / below show you how to pronounce the Spanish words. The syllable after the apostrophe ' is stressed).

(1) there exist two ways to pronounce the letter 'C'. **Ce** and **ci** are pronounced /θ/; **ca**, **co** and **cu** /k/, though.

EXAMPLES:

casa /'kasa/	house
cebolla /θe'bɒja/	onion
cigarro /θi'garrɒ/	cigarette
coche /'kɒtʃe/	car
cuna /'kʊna/	crib

‚Ch' is, as in English, pronounced /tʃ/.

EXAMPLES:

chico	boy
chica	girl
chocolate	chocolate

(2) **ga**, **go** and **gu** are pronounced /ga/, /gɒ/, /gʊ/. But: **ge** /he/ and **gi** /hi/.

The words pronounced /ge/ and /gi/ are written slightly different, namely **gue** and **gui**.

EXAMPLES:

gato /'gatɒ/	cat
guerra /'gerra/	war
guitarra /gi'tarra/	guitar
golf /gɒlf/	golf
gusano /gʊ'sanɒ/	worm

but...
Gerardo /he'rardɒ/	(*male first name*)
giro /'hirɒ/	turn, spin

In Spanish you can find certain words where the letter groups **gue** and **gui** are actually pronounced /gʊe/ and /gʊi/. To distinguish these cases, such words are written with the special vowel **ü**.

Compare the different pronunciations here:

guía /'gia/   guide
pingüino /pin'gʊinɒ/[3]   penguin

guepardo /ge'pardɒ/   cheetah
paragüero /para'gʊerɒ/[4]   umbrella stand

(3) The letter 'h' is <u>not</u> spoken in Spanish. Exception: when 'h' is preceded by a 'c' (pronunciation rule 1).

EXAMPLE:

hora /'ɒra/   hour, time[5]

(4) ‚ll' is not pronounced /l/ (!!!), but /j/ (Advanced tip ▶▶: the vocal chords vibrate, i.e. it is a voiced sound).

*So, next time you order paella, remember it's **/Pa'eja/**, not /Pa'ela/.*

Advanced **tip** ▶▶

The sounds of 'y' and 'll' are mixed by many native speakers (this phenomenon is called *yeísmo*), and are pronounced as /j/ -the pronunciation for 'y' as in "yellow"-.

(5) Advanced **tip** ▶▶

'ñ' (n with tilde over it) is a unique letter, it does not belong to the Latin alphabet. The pronunciation is very similar to the word "canyon". It is also a voiced sound.

(6) 'q' is <u>always</u> followed by "u", but this "u" is <u>not</u> pronounced.

EXAMPLE:

---

[3] not /pin'ginɒ/
[4] not /para'gerɒ/
[5] In the question "What time is it?" (see the vocabulary section "The time")

máquina /'makina/   machine

(7) it gets a little tricky. On one hand there is 'rr', and on the other hand 'r'.

Advanced tip ▶▶

To pronounce 'r', place the tip of the tongue on the oral cavity behind the upper teeth and gently caress the teeth while blowing out. For 'rr', the same tip as for 'r', but with vibration of the vocal chords (the sound is like from a chainsaw).

→   Exception: 'r' at the beginning of the word is pronounced like 'rr'.

EXAMPLES:

Roma /'rrɒma/   Rome
caro /'karɒ/   expensive
correr /kɒ'rrer/   run

(8) Advanced tip ▶▶

The 's' is pronounced /θ/ in Andalusia (southern Spain). This phenomenon is called *ceceo*.

(9) Advanced tip ▶▶

The sounds of the letters 'v' and 'b' are mixed even by many native speakers. As a result, the words *baca* (**roof luggage rack**) and *vaca* (cow) become homophones (pronounced the same way). However, the meanings of the two words are completely different.

(10) This letter is pronunced /s/ in South America, the Canary Islands and Andalusia -the phenomenon is called *seseo*-.

Vowels

a   **e**   **i**   **o**   **u**

ü exists as mentioned above (pronunciation rule 2).

The Spanish vowels carry a graphic accent (called *tilde*) in certain cases (**á, é, í, ó, ú**). For simplification, it could be said that these appear in stressed syllables, provided the rules of accentuation are fulfilled.

árbol	tree
beb**é**	baby
r**í**o	river
cami**ó**n	lorry, truck
seg**ú**n	according to

Advanced tip ▶▶

<u>Rules of accentuation</u>

The following basic rules are applied:

1. Words with the stress on the last syllable and those ending in vowel, -n or -s *(agudas)*

   EXAMPLE: cortés   polite

2. Words stressed on the penultimate syllable and ending on consonants (except -n or -s) *(llanas)*

   EXAMPLE: difícil   difficult, hard

3. Words stressed on the third or fourth last syllable (regardless of the ending) *(esdrújulas)*

   EXAMPLE: húmedo   humid

Other special rules apply when writing two vowels in a row which do not belong to the same syllable (e.g. *río*). For simplicity reasons, I will not go into this in more detail here.

Consonants

The rest of the letters: **b c d f g h j k l m n ñ p q r s t v w x y z**

Grammar

Articles

In Spanish we have 2 genders: masculine or feminine.

Indefinite articles

	Singular	Plural
Masculine	un	unos
Feminine	una	unas

Definite articles

	Singular	Plural
Masculine	el	los
Feminine	la	las

EXAMPLES:

El libro es muy bueno.   The book is very good.

La casa es grande.   The house is big.

Tenéis **unos** amigos ahí.   You have some friends there.

Subject pronouns

yo	I
tú	you
él	he
ella	she
	it[6]
usted	you (*formal*)
nosotros	we (*masc.*)
nosotras	we (*fem.*)

---

[6] In Spanish, 'it' does not have a direct equivalent; instead, verbs are conjugated in the third person singular and the subject is implied.

vosotros	you (*plural*)
ustedes	you (*plural, formal*)
ellos	they (*masc.*)
ellas	they (*fem.*)

„Usted/ustedes" are the formal pronouns for „you". „Vosotros" is widely used in Spain except in the Canary Islands and Andalusia, here and in South America they prefer to use „ustedes".

Possessive pronouns

mi (*sing.*) / **mis** (*pl.*)	my
tu (*sing.*) / **tus** (*pl.*)	your
su (*sing.*) / **sus** (*pl.*)	his/her/its
nuestro (*masc.*) / **nuestra** (*fem.*)	our
vuestro (*masc.*) / **vuestra** (*fem.*)	your
su (*sing.*) / **sus** (*pl.*)	their

Interrogative pronouns

¿Qué?	What?
¿Quién?, ¿quiénes? (*pl.*)	Who?
¿A quién?	Whom?
¿Cuándo?	When?
¿Cuánto?	How many / How much?
¿Por qué?	Why?
¿Dónde?	Where?
¿Cómo?	How?
¿Cuál?, ¿Cuáles? (*pl.*)	Which?

Please notice that these pronouns may as well be used in declarative sentences, but without the accent.

EXAMPLES:

Esa es la casa **donde** vivo.

That is the house **where** I live.

Esa es la casa **que** quiero.

That is the house **that** I want.

Me gusta viajar **porque**[7] me siento libre.

I like travelling, **because** I feel free.

Tenses

In this book, the verbs are conjugated in these 5 tenses:

✓ *PRESENTE (PRESENT SIMPLE)*
   Action in the present

(Yo[8]) **vivo** en Australia.

I **live** in Australia.

✓ *PRETÉRITO PERFECTO COMPUESTO (PRESENT PERFECT)*
   Action recently or just completed

Has desayunado mucho hoy.

You **have eaten** a lot for breakfast *today*.

✓ *PRETÉRITO PERFECTO SIMPLE (PAST SIMPLE)*
   Action in the past completed → no connection to the present

Ella **trabajó** ayer.

She **worked** yesterday (*so it is over*).

✓ *PRETÉRITO IMPERFECTO (IMPERFECT)*
   Recurring action that occurred in the past

Él **jugaba** a fútbol cada semana.

He **used to play** football *every week*.

✓ *FUTURO (SIMPLE FUTURE)*
   Actions occurs in the future

---

[7] "porque" written in one word! (unlike "por qué")

[8] The subject pronoun "yo" may be omitted because it's evident that it is ME (1st person) who lives in Australia, since the verb "vivo" is the conjugation used exclusively for the 1st person singular.

Mañana yo **comeré** pasta.   Tomorrow I **will eat** pasta.

Verbs „ser/estar"

Both correspond to the verb „to be". In Spanish we differentiate between
„ser" and „estar". The conjugations of both in present simple, present
perfect, past simple, imperfect and future simple:

PRESENT SIMPLE

	Ser	*Estar*	ENG
Yo	**soy**	**estoy**	I am
Tú	**eres**	**estás**	you are
Él/ella | usted	**es**	**está**	He/she is | you are
Nosotros	**somos**	**estamos**	We are
Vosotros	**sois**	**estáis**	You are
Ellos/ellas | ustedes	**son**	**están**	They are | you are

PRESENT PERFECT

	Ser	*Estar*	ENG
Yo	**he sido**	**he estado**	I have been
Tú	**has sido**	**has estado**	You have been
Él/ella | usted	**ha sido**	**ha estado**	He/she has been | you have been
Nosotros	**hemos sido**	**hemos estado**	We have been
Vosotros	**habéis sido**	**habéis estado**	You have been
Ellos/ellas | ustedes	**han sido**	**han estado**	They | you have been

PAST SIMPLE

	Ser	*Estar*	ENG
Yo	**fui**	**estuve**	I was

Tú	fuiste	estuviste	You were
Él/ella | usted	fue	estuvo	He/she was | you were
Nosotros	fuimos	estuvimos	We were
Vosotros	fuisteis	estuvisteis	You were
Ellos/ellas | ustedes	fueron	estuvieron	They | you were

IMPERFECT

	Ser	*Estar*	ENG
Yo	era	estaba	I used to be
Tú	eras	estabas	You used to be
Él/ella | usted	era	estaba	He/she used to be | you used to be
Nosotros	éramos	estábamos	We used to be
Vosotros	erais	estabais	You used to be
Ellos/ellas | ustedes	eran	estaban	They | you used to be

The imperfect tense (used to) can be translated into Spanish as "solía" + verb in infinitive:

Yo	solía
Tú	solías
Él/ella/usted	solía
Nosotros	solíamos
Vosotros	solíais
Ellos/ellas/ustedes	solían

EXAMPLE:

Yo **solía** cenar a las 8 de la noche.   I **used to** have dinner at 8 pm.

	Ser	Estar	ENG
Yo	**seré**	**estaré**	I will be
Tú	**serás**	**estarás**	You will be
Él/ella | usted	**será**	**estará**	He/she | you will be
Nosotros	**seremos**	**estaremos**	We will be
Vosotros	**seréis**	**estaréis**	You will be
Ellos/ellas | ustedes	**serán**	**estarán**	They will be | you will be

Differences between „ser" and „estar"

In general, the main difference is this: *ser* describes a permanent property of someone or something, whereas *estar* indicates a temporary state.

Ser
Uses

- Personal introduction
  (Yo) **soy** Pedro.   My name **is** Pedro.

- Time, date, day
  Hoy **es** lunes, 3 de octubre.   Today **is** Monday, October 3rd.
  ¿Qué hora **es**? **Son** las tres de la tarde.   What**'s** the time? It**'s** 3 pm.

- Possession
  Ese **es** mi ordenador.   That**'s** my computer.

- Origin
  (Yo) **soy** español.   I**'m** Spanish. / I **am** a Spaniard.

- Descriptions
  Soy alto.   I**'m** tall.
  La mesa **es** grande.   The table **is** big.

- Passive voice
  El español **es hablado** en Chile.   Spanish **is spoken** in Chile.

Estar
Uses

- Location of a place, object or person
  Estoy en Francia.   I**'m** in France.

- Temporary states
  Estoy cansado.   I**'m** tired.
  Estaré feliz allí.   I**'ll be** happy there.

- Continuous tenses
  Estoy escribiendo un libro.   I**'m** writing a book.

Verbs „haber/tener"

Haber: there is/are, have (modal verb for the construction of present perfect)

Tener: have (=possess)

PRESENT SIMPLE

	Haber	*Tener*	ENG
Yo	**he**	**tengo**	I have
Tú	**has**	**tienes**	You have
Él/ella | usted	**ha**	**tiene**	He/she has | you have
Ø *(no pronoun!)*	**hay**		There is/are
Nosotros	**hemos**	**tenemos**	We have
Vosotros	**habéis**	**tenéis**	You have
Ellos/ellas | ustedes	**han**	**tienen**	They | you have

PRESENT PERFECT

	Haber	*Tener*	ENG
Yo		**he tenido**	I have had
Tú		**has tenido**	You have had
Él/ella | usted		**ha tenido**	He/she has | you have had
Ø	**ha habido**		There has/have been
Nosotros		**hemos tenido**	We have had
Vosotros		**habéis tenido**	You have had
Ellos/ellas | ustedes		**han tenido**	They | you have had

PAST SIMPLE

	Haber	Tener	ENG
Yo	**hube**	**tuve**	I had
Tú	**hubiste**	**tuviste**	You had
Él/ella | usted	**hubo**	**tuvo**	He/she | you had
Ø	**hubo**		There was/were
Nosotros	**hubimos**	**tuvimos**	We had
Vosotros	**hubisteis**	**tuvisteis**	You had
Ellos/ellas | ustedes	**hubieron**	**tuvieron**	They | you had

IMPERFECT

	Haber	Tener	ENG
Yo	**había**	**tenía**	I had
Tú	**habías**	**tenías**	You had
Él/ella | usted	**había**	**tenía**	He/she | you had
Ø	**había**		There was/were
Nosotros	**habíamos**	**teníamos**	We had
Vosotros	**habíais**	**teníais**	You had
Ellos/ellas | ustedes	**habían**	**tenían**	They | you had

FUTURE SIMPLE

	Haber	Tener	ENG
Yo	**habré**	**tendré**	I will have
Tú	**habrás**	**tendrás**	You will have
Él/ella | usted	**habrá**	**tendrá**	He/she | you will have
Ø	**habrá**		There will be
Nosotros	**habremos**	**tendremos**	We will have
Vosotros	**habréis**	**tendréis**	You will have
Ellos/ellas | ustedes	**habrán**	**tendrán**	They | you will have

Tener que or *haber que* (only in the 3ʳᵈ person singular) are used in Spanish to mark the obligation to complete a task (have to, must). The constructs are synonyms of *deber*.

EXAMPLES:

Yo **habré** comido con ellos. *I will have eaten with them.*

Hay grandes descuentos en ese supermercado. *There are huge discounts at the supermarket.*

Tienes que contarme esa historia. *You have to tell me that story.*

Hay que salir rápido, antes de que vuelva Pedro. *We must go quickly, before Pedro comes back.*

¿**Tuvieron** ellos un coche rojo cuando vivían en Mallorca? *Did they have a red car when they lived in Mallorca?*

Other modal verbs

✓ Can

Puedo hacer esto. I **can** do this.

✓ Could

No **pude** dejar de reírme. I **could**n't help laughing.

✓ Would

Yo **me atrevería** a hablar. I **would dare** to speak up.

✓ Will / shall

¿Te **vas a** callar, por favor? **Will** you please **shut up**?
¿**Vamos** al cinema entonces? **Shall** we **go** to the cinema then?

✓ Should / ought to

Debería ir al medico. I **should** go to the doctor's.

Deberías escucharle. You **ought to** listen to her.

✓ May / might

Es posible que cante.   He **may** sing.

Puede que llueva hoy.   It **might** rain today.

✓ Need (*semi-modal*)

No necesitas explicarlo.   You **needn't** explain it.

Verbs „traer/llevar"
Traer: bring   *Llevar*: take

PRESENT SIMPLE

	traer	*llevar*	ENG
Yo	**traigo**	**llevo**	I bring/take
Tú	**traes**	**llevas**	You bring/take
Él/ella | usted	**trae**	**lleva**	He/she brings/takes | You bring/take
Nosotros	**traemos**	**llevamos**	We bring/take
Vosotros	**traéis**	**lleváis**	You bring/take
Ellos/ellas | ustedes	**traen**	**llevan**	They | you bring/take

PRESENT PERFECT

	traer	*llevar*	ENG
Yo	**he traído**	**he llevado**	I have brought/ taken
Tú	**has traído**	**has llevado**	You have brought/ taken
Él/ella | usted	**ha traído**	**ha llevado**	He/she has | you have brought/ taken
Nosotros	**hemos traído**	**hemos llevado**	We have brought/ taken
Vosotros	**habéis traído**	**habéis llevado**	You have brought/taken
Ellos/ellas | ustedes	**han traído**	**han llevado**	They | you have brought/taken

PAST SIMPLE

	traer	llevar	ENG
Yo	**traje**	**llevé**	I brought/took
Tú	**trajiste**	**llevaste**	You brought/took
Él/ella | usted	**trajo**	**llevó**	He/she | you brought/took
Nosotros	**trajimos**	**llevamos**	We brought/took
Vosotros	**trajisteis**	**llevasteis**	You brought/took
Ellos/ellas | ustedes	**trajeron**	**llevaron**	They | you brought/took

IMPERFECT

	traer	llevar	ENG
Yo	**traía**	**llevaba**	I used to bring/take
Tú	**traías**	**llevabas**	You used to bring/take
Él/ella | usted	**traía**	**llevaba**	He/she | you used to bring/take
Nosotros	**traíamos**	**llevábamos**	We used to bring/ take
Vosotros	**traíais**	**llevabais**	You used to bring/ take
Ellos/ellas | ustedes	**traían**	**llevaban**	They | you used to bring/take

FUTURE SIMPLE

	traer	llevar	ENG
Yo	**traeré**	**llevaré**	I will bring/take
Tú	**traerás**	**llevarás**	You will bring/take
Él/ella | usted	**traerá**	**llevará**	He/she | you will bring/take
Nosotros	**traeremos**	**llevaremos**	We will bring/take
Vosotros	**traeréis**	**llevaréis**	You will bring/take
Ellos/ellas | ustedes	**traerán**	**llevarán**	They | you will bring/take

Verbs „ir/venir"

ir: go   *venir*: come

PRESENT SIMPLE

	ir	*venir*	ENG
Yo	**voy**	**vengo**	I go/come
Tú	**vas**	**vienes**	You go/come
Él/ella | usted	**va**	**viene**	He/she goes/comes | you go
Nosotros	**vamos**	**venimos**	We go/come
Vosotros	**vais**	**venís**	You go/come
Ellos/ellas | ustedes	**van**	**vienen**	They | you go/come

PRESENT PERFECT

	ir	*venir*	ENG
Yo	**he ido**	**he venido**	I have gone/come
Tú	**has ido**	**has venido**	You have gone/ come
Él/ella | usted	**ha ido**	**ha venido**	He/she has | you have gone/ come
Nosotros	**hemos ido**	**hemos venido**	We have gone/ come
Vosotros	**habéis ido**	**habéis venido**	You have gone/ come
Ellos/ellas | ustedes	**han ido**	**han venido**	They | you have gone/come

PAST SIMPLE

	ir	*venir*	ENG
Yo	**fui**	**vine**	I went/came
Tú	**fuiste**	**viniste**	you went/came
Él/ella | usted	**fue**	**vino**	he/she | you went/came

Nosotros	**fuimos**	**vinimos**	we went/came
Vosotros	**fuisteis**	**vinisteis**	you went/came
Ellos/ellas | ustedes	**fueron**	**vinieron**	they | you went/came

IMPERFECT

	ir	*venir*	ENG
Yo	**iba**	**venía**	I used to go/come
Tú	**ibas**	**venías**	You used to go/ come
Él/ella | usted	**iba**	**venía**	He/she | you used to go/come
Nosotros	**íbamos**	**veníamos**	We used to go/ come
Vosotros	**ibais**	**veníais**	You used to go/ come
Ellos/ellas | ustedes	**iban**	**venían**	They | you used to go/come

FUTURE SIMPLE

	ir	*venir*	ENG
Yo	**iré**	**vendré**	I will go/come
Tú	**irás**	**vendrás**	You will go/come
Él/ella | usted	**irá**	**vendrá**	He/she | you will go/come
Nosotros	**iremos**	**vendremos**	We will go/come
Vosotros	**iréis**	**vendréis**	You will go/come
Ellos/ellas | ustedes	**irán**	**vendrán**	They | you will go/ come

Conjugations -ar,-er,-ir

The Spanish verbs in infinitive end in -ar, -er or -ir. Most verbs with these endings are conjugated the same way. As an example, we take the verbs *hablar* (talk), *comer* (eat) and *vivir* (live).

PRESENT SIMPLE

	Hablar	Comer	vivir
Yo	hablo	como	vivo
Tú	hablas	comes	vives
Él/ella/usted	habla	come	vive
Nosotros	hablamos	comemos	vivimos
Vosotros	habláis	coméis	vivís
Ellos/ellas/ustedes	hablan	comen	viven

PRESENT PERFECT

	Hablar	Comer	vivir
Yo	he hablado	he comido	he vivido
Tú	has hablado	has comido	has vivido
Él/ella/usted	ha hablado	ha comido	ha vivido
Nosotros	hemos hablado	hemos comido	hemos vivido
Vosotros	habéis hablado	habéis comido	habéis vivido
Ellos/ellas/ustedes	han hablado	han comido	han vivido

PAST SIMPLE

	Hablar	Comer	vivir
Yo	hablé	comí	viví
Tú	hablaste	comiste	viviste
Él/ella/usted	habló	comió	vivió
Nosotros	hablamos	comimos	vivimos
Vosotros	hablasteis	comisteis	vivisteis
Ellos/ellas/ustedes	hablaron	comieron	vivieron

IMPERFECT

	Hablar	Comer	vivir

Yo	**habl**aba	**com**ía	**viv**ía
Tú	**habl**abas	**com**ías	**viv**ías
Él/ella/usted	**habl**aba	**com**ía	**viv**ía
Nosotros	**habl**ábamos	**com**íamos	**viv**íamos
Vosotros	**habl**abais	**com**íais	**viv**íais
Ellos/ellas/ustedes	**habl**aban	**com**ían	**viv**ían

FUTURE SIMPLE

	Hablar	*Comer*	*vivir*
Yo	**habl**aré	**com**eré	**viv**iré
Tú	**habl**arás	**com**erás	**viv**irás
Él/ella/usted	**habl**ará	**com**erá	**viv**irá
Nosotros	**habl**aremos	**com**eremos	**viv**iremos
Vosotros	**habl**aréis	**com**eréis	**viv**ireis
Ellos/ellas/ustedes	**habl**arán	**com**erán	**viv**irán

Reflexive Verbs

To form a reflexive verb, the particle *"se"* is added. For example, the verb *ducharse* (have a shower). Simply place the pronoun in front of the verb, the verb *ducharse* is conjugated like the -ar verbs.

PRESENT SIMPLE

	Ducharse
Yo	*me* **ducho**
Tú	*te* **duchas**
Él/ella/usted	*se* **ducha**
Nosotros	*nos* **duchamos**
Vosotros	*os* **ducháis**
Ellos/ellas/ustedes	*se* **duchan**

PRESENT PERFECT

	Ducharse
Yo	**me he duchado**
Tú	**te has duchado**
Él/ella/usted	**se ha duchado**
Nosotros	**nos hemos duchado**
Vosotros	**os habéis duchado**
Ellos/ellas/Ustedes	**se han duchado**

PAST SIMPLE

	Ducharse
Yo	**me duché**
Tú	**te duchaste**
Él/ella/usted	**se duchó**
Nosotros	**nos duchamos**
Vosotros	**os duchasteis**
Ellos/ellas/ustedes	**se ducharon**

IMPERFECT

	Ducharse
Yo	**me duchaba**
Tú	**te duchabas**
Él/ella/usted	**se duchaba**
Nosotros	**nos duchábamos**
Vosotros	**os duchabais**
Ellos/ellas/ustedes	**se duchaban**

FUTURE SIMPLE

	Ducharse
Yo	**me ducharé**
Tú	**te ducharás**
Él/ella/usted	**se duchará**

Nosotros	**nos ducharemos**
Vosotros	**os ducharéis**
Ellos/ellas/ustedes	**se ducharán**

Negation

The negation in Spanish is quite simple. You use the word "no" as a negative answer to a yes-no question or to negate the verb.

EXAMPLES:

A: **¿Te gusta este piso?**	Do you like this flat?
B: *No*, **es bastante feo.**	No, it's quite ugly.
No **he dormido mucho.**	I haven't slept much.

1	**Hola, me llamo John.**	Hello, my name is John.
2	**¿Qué tal está?**	How do you do?
	¿Qué tal estás?	How are you doing?
3	**Muy bien, gracias.**	Fine, thanks.
4	**De nada.**	You're welcome/My pleasure.
5	**Hablo un poco de español.**	I speak a little Spanish.
6	**¿Puede repetir?**	Could you please repeat?
7	**Más despacio, por favor.**	More slowly, please.
8	**Disculpe, quiero una cerveza, por favor.**	Excuse me, I'd like a beer, please.
9	**Hace frío/calor aquí.**	It's cold/hot here.
10	**No entiendo.**	I don't understand.
11	**Soy inglés** (fem. **inglesa**).	I'm English.
	Soy americano/a (fem.).	I'm American.
12	**Lo siento.**	I'm sorry.
13	**Adiós.**	Goodbye.
14	**¿Cuánto cuesta eso?**	How much is that?
15	**¿Qué significa...?**	What does ... mean?
16	**Mucho gusto / Encantado/a** (fem.).	Nice/Pleased to meet you.
17	**Necesito ayuda, por favor.**	I need some help, please.
18	**Buenos días.**	Good morning.
19	**Buenas tardes.**	Good afternoon.
20	**Buenas noches.**	Good evening/night.

The numbers

1 uno	17 diecisiete	40 cuarenta
2 dos	18 dieciocho	50 cincuenta
3 tres	19 diecinueve	60 sesenta
4 cuatro	20 veinte	70 setenta
5 cinco	21 veintiuno	80 ochenta
6 seis	22 veintidós	90 noventa
7 siete	23 veintitrés	100 cien
8 ocho	24 veinticuatro	101 ciento uno
9 nueve	25 veinticinco	102 ciento dos
10 diez	26 veintiséis	110 ciento diez
11 once	27 veintisiete	200 doscientos
12 doce	28 veintiocho	1000 mil
13 trece	29 veintinueve	10000 diez mil
14 catorce	30 treinta	100000 cien mil
15 quince	31 treinta y uno	1000000 un millón
16 dieciséis	32 treinta y dos	

To form the other numbers, you simply have to split them into parts and then pronounce the parts separately. So:

1286 - **mil doscientos ochenta y seis**

Beware! The numbers from 31 to 99 are written slightly different than in English. The ten and unit are not joined by a dash, but by the conjunction *y* (and):

63 sesenta **y** tres (sixty-three)

Exception: the numbers 21 to 29 are combined in one word.

23 **veintitrés** (not "veinte y tres").

The years and the numbers are formed in the same way (so no year "diecinueve noventa y tres (nineteen ninety-three)").

Ordinal numbers

1° primero	14° decimocuarto
2° segundo	20° vigésimo
3° tercero	21° vigésimo primero
4° cuarto	22° vigésimo segundo
5° quinto	30° trigésimo
6° sexto	40° cuadragésimo
7° séptimo	50° quincuagésimo
8° octavo	60° sexagésimo
9° noveno	70° septuagésimo
10° décimo	80° octogésimo
11° decimoprimero	90° nonagésimo
12° decimosegundo	100° centésimo
13° decimotercero	1000° milésimo

Days of the week

lunes	Monday
martes	Tuesday
miércoles	Wednesday
jueves	Thursday

viernes	Friday
sábado	Saturday
domingo	Sunday

The week begins on Mondays.

The months

enero	January
febrero	February
marzo	March
abril	April
mayo	May
junio	June
julio	July
agosto	August
septiembre	September
octubre	October
noviembre	November
diciembre	December

The seasons

primavera	spring
verano	summer
otoño	autumn
invierno	winter

The colours

blanco	white
negro	black
rojo	red
amarillo	yellow
verde	green
marrón	brown
lila	lilac
violeta	purple
azul	blue
rosa	pink
gris	grey
naranja	orange
azul claro/celeste	light blue
azul marino	navy
verde azulado	teal
turquesa	turquoise

The time

What time is it?	**¿Qué hora es?**
It is…	**Son las…, es la…** (*just between 12:35 and 13:30*), **es…** (*for midday/midnight*)
9:00	**las nueve (en punto)**
9:10	**las nueve y diez**
9:15	**las nueve y cuarto**
9:20	**las nueve y veinte**
9:25	**las nueve y veinticinco**

9:30	**las nueve y media**
9:35	**las <u>diez</u> menos veinticinco**
9:40	**las diez menos veinte**
9:45	**las diez menos cuarto**
9:50	**las diez menos diez**
9:55	**las diez menos cinco**
13:00	**la una (en punto)**
13:15	**la una y cuarto**
12:55	**la una menos cinco**
12:00 pm	**mediodía**
12:00 am	**medianoche**

In spite of the oddity, it is also possible to say the exact minutes (usually rounded up or down to the next 5-minute cut):

| 4:13 | **las cuatro y trece (minutos)** |

To differentiate the hours of the morning, afternoon or evening (should it not be obvious to the other person), add the part of the day accordingly. 20:15 las ocho y cuarto de la tarde

23:10 las once y diez **de la noche**

10:30 las diez y media **de la mañana**

Exercises & games – Ejercicios y juegos

1.   ¿Qué hora es?

6:15 Son las ...

14:00

19:50

13:05

15:35

12:00 (midday)

2. Hoy es... (*Write the numbers in words*)

e.g.:
0. Saturday, 11th April 2004 **sábado, 11 de abril de 2004 / sábado, once de abril de dos mil cuatro**

Friday, 1st March 2019

Friday, 8th July 2007

Sunday, 4th August 1965

Tuesday, 23rd December 1986

3. Fill in the gaps.

A: Hola, _______ (*to be*) María. Mucho gusto. Y tú, ¿cómo te llamas?

B: ____________ Juan Carlos.

¿________ es esa chica? ______ es Sara (*she*).

¿_______ cansado? _____ (*negation*), me encuentro bien.

Yo hoy com_ jamón.

Mañana empezar____ a correr.

<u>Vocabulary</u>	
empezar	begin, start
encontrarse	feel

4. Record yourself! <u>It is scientifically proven that people can store more information when they hear than when they simply read</u>. The recordings are best played back just before you go to bed. This is the time when the brain is most receptive. You will be surprised how much you improve after listening to the recordings several nights (without interruption).

5. Create flashcards for the vocabulary you learn in this book. Write the word on the front and the translation in English or, ideally, a drawing or a photo that reminds you of this word on the back. After the flashcards are created, you can study them multiple times (define the timeframe when you study, according to your rhythm: every few days, weeks...), this way, you effectively anchor this vocabulary in your long-term memory.

6. Put stickers on the refrigerator, closet, doors... with relevant vocabulary in Spanish and its meaning. This way you can see them more often and memorize them faster.

Level 2

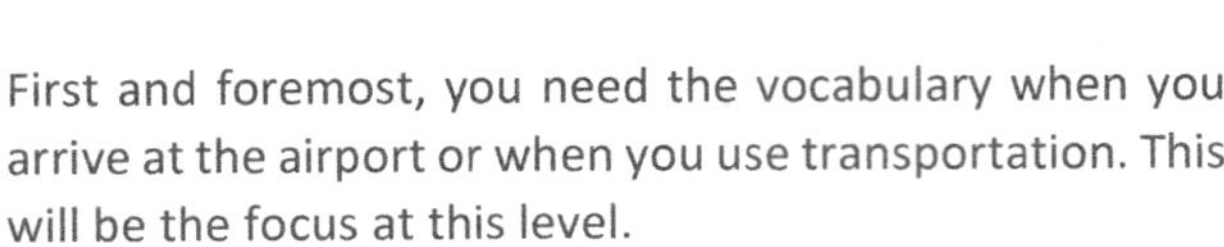

5

First and foremost, you need the vocabulary when you arrive at the airport or when you use transportation. This will be the focus at this level.

At the airport – En el aeropuerto

Top phrases

¿Dónde está la salida?	Where is the exit?
Su pasaporte, por favor.	Your passport, please.
¿Cuántas maletas quiere facturar?	How many items of baggage would you like to check in?
¿Tiene un número de reserva?	Have you got a booking number?
Estoy de viaje de negocios.	I'm on a business trip.
Estoy de vacaciones.	I'm on vacation/holidays.
¿Va mi vuelo con retraso?	Is my flight delayed?
¿Cuál es mi puerta de embarque, por favor?	What is my boarding gate, please?

At the check-in counter

aeropuerto	Airport
equipaje	Baggage/Luggage
equipaje de mano	Hand luggage
facturar	Check in
límite de equipaje	Baggage allowance
llegadas	Arrivals
maleta	Suitcase
mostrador de facturación	Check-in counter
peso	Weight

reserva	Booking
salidas	Departures
tarjeta de embarque	Boarding pass
visa/visado	Visa

At the customs

¿Tiene algo que declarar?	Do you have anything to declare?
aduana	Customs
artículos	Goods
cantidades permitidas para viajar	Travel allowances
declarar	Declare
Me han perdido mi equipaje.	My luggage was lost.
Me han robado el equipaje.	My luggage was stolen.
Mi maleta tiene daños.	My suitcase is damaged.

Baggage

cinta de equipajes	baggage carousel
dimensiones (de la maleta)	Luggage dimensions
equipaje deportivo	Sports baggage
objetos peligrosos	Dangerous objects
recogida de equipajes	Baggage reclaim
sobrepeso	Overweight

On the plane

a bordo	On board
abrocharse el cinturón de seguridad	Fasten the seat belt
asiento	seat
aterrizar	land
avión	plane
azafato/azafata	flight attendant

baño	lavatory
clase business	Business class
clase turista	Tourist class
despegar	Take off
pasillo	Aisle
piloto	Pilot
salida de emergencia	Emergency exit
tripulación	Crew
turbulencias	turbulences
vuelo	flight

Means of transportation – Medios de transporte

Bus

¿A dónde viaja este autobús?	Where does this bus drive?
autobús	bus
autocar	coach
billete	ticket
conductor de autobús/chófer	bus driver
dinero suelto	change
estación de autobuses	bus station
horarios	timetables
maletero	baggage compartment
marquesina	bus shelter
parada	bus stop

Train

Andén	Platform
Anuncio por megafonía	Train announcement
Bajar del tren	Get off the train
Billete de ida	One-way ticket
Billete de ida y vuelta	Round ticket
Estación central	Central station
Estación de tren	Railway station

Hacer transbordo	change trains	
Pasajero	passenger	
Primera clase	1st class	
Retraso	Delay	
Revisor	Conductor	
Segunda clase	2nd class	
Su billete, por favor.	Your ticket, please.	
Subir al tren	Board the train	
Taquilla	Counter	
Tren	Train	
Tren de cercanías	Suburban railway	
Tren nocturno	Night train	
Vagón restaurante	Wagon-restaurant	
Vagón/coche	coach	
Vía	track	

Taxi

¿A dónde le llevo?	Where would you like to go?
¿Cuánto se tarda en llegar?	How long does it take to get there?
La dirección es…	The address is…
Maletero	Carrying case
Recibo	receipt
Tarifa	Tariff
Taxímetro	taximeter
Taxista	Taxi driver

Car

¿Cuánto cuesta el alquiler por día/semana?	How much is the rent per day/week?
¿Dónde está la gasolinera más próxima?	Where is the nearest petrol/gas station?
¿Se puede aparcar aquí?	Is it allowed to park here?
accidente	accident
acelerador	throttle

aire acondicionado	air conditioning	
atasco	traffic jam	
autopista	Motorway/highway	
cambio automático	Automatic	
cambio manual	manual gearbox	
carril	Track	
coche, carro	Car	
conductor	Car driver	
copiloto	Copilot	
El coche tiene un pinchazo.	The car has a flat tire.	
embrague	Clutch	
estación de servicio	Rest stop, motorway service area	
Estoy buscando un parking.	I'm looking for a parking garage.	
freno	Brake	
freno de mano	Handbrake	
marcha	Gear	
marcha atrás	Reverse gear	
meter una marcha	engage a gear	
Mi coche está averiado.	My car has broken down.	
palanca de cambios	Gearshift	
parquímetro	Parking meter	
peaje	Toll, toll station	
Quiero alquilar un coche.	I want to rent a car.	
quitar una marcha	Shift down a gear	
retrovisor	Rearview mirror/exterior mirror	
salida	exit	
seguro	Insurance	
semáforo	traffic light	
volante	handlebars	

At the petrol station

¿A cuánto está el litro de gasolina/diesel?	How much does petrol/diesel cost per litre?
gasolina	gasoline, petrol
gasolinera	petrol station

Lleno, por favor.   Fill it full, please.
repostar   Fill up the tank
sin plomo   unleaded
surtidor (de gasolina)   Petrol pump

Tram
tranvía   tram
raíles   rails

Underground/subway
¿Cuál es el camino más corto
para ir a...?   What is the shortest way to ...?
línea (de metro)   Underground/subway line
metro   Underground/subway
plano de metro   Underground map
próxima parada   Next stop
Tarjeta transporte   Travelcard
torno   Turning machine

Bike
bicicleta   bike
bomba, inflador   air pump
cadena   bicycle chain
cámara de aire   hose
candado   lock
cantimplora   drinking bottle
casco   helmet
faro   lamp
freno delantero   front wheel brake
freno trasero   rear wheel brake
manillar   handlebars
pedales   pedals
rueda delantera   front wheel

| **rueda trasera** | rear wheel |
| **sillín** | saddle |

Boat

amarrar	moor
barco	ship
camarote	cabin
capitán	captain
desembarcar	leave the ship
embarcar	embark
ferry	ferry
muelle	dock
puerto	port, harbour
zarpar	sail away

Exercises & games

1. Find 15 words of this level in the word search puzzle. Note: the last letter of a word can also be the same as the first letter of another word.

Llegada

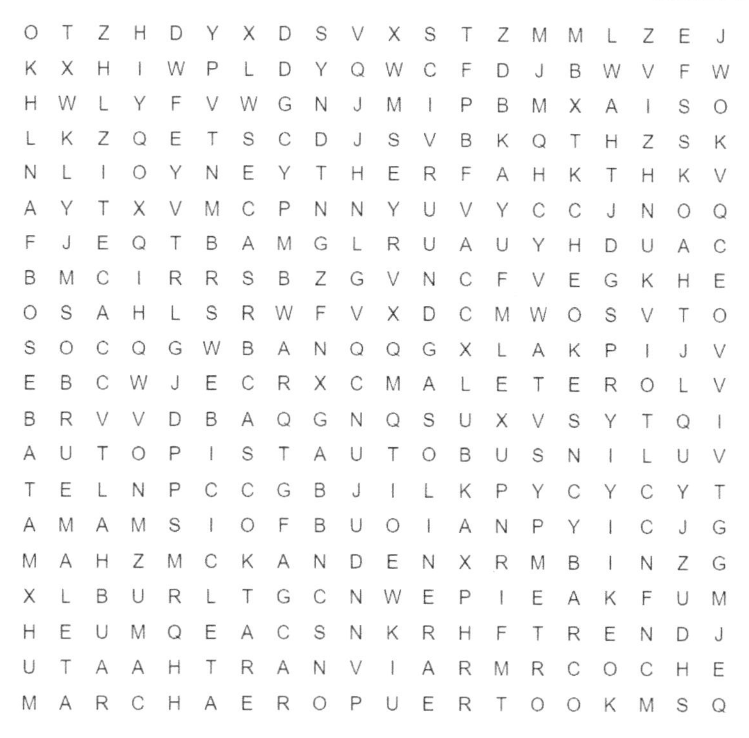

Source: www.educima.com

2. Translate the following words of this level:

bike   _______________________________

car   _______________________________

petrol   _______________________

train   _______________________

flight attendant   _______________________

bus   _______________________

bus driver   _______________________

air conditioning   _______________________

toll   _______________________

insurance   _______________________

3. Fill in the gaps with words of this level:

Estoy en el aeropuerto. Mi _________ despega a las 18 h.

Quiero alquilar un _______ barato.

Necesito _________ gasolina. ¿Dónde está la ___________ más próxima?

Ya he ___________ mi maleta. Ahora estoy buscando la _________________.

Tengo sed, necesito una __________________ llena de agua.

> Vocabulary
> **barato**   cheap
> **sed**   thrist
> **necesitar**   need

Level 3
Accommodation

6

You are finally in your holiday destination, you surely want to drop off your luggage now and relax. Enclosed are the speaking resources regarding the accommodation:

Top phrases

Tengo una reserva a nombre de...	I have a reservation in the name of...
¿Me puede dar un mapa (de la ciudad), por favor?	Could you give me a city map, please?
¿Está el desayuno incluido?	Is the breakfast included?
¿En qué planta está mi habitación?	What floor is my room on?
¿Cuál es la contraseña del wifi?	Could you please give me the Wifi password?

Searching

¿A qué distancia se encuentra el hotel del casco antiguo?	How far is the hotel from the old town?
¿Cuáles son los gastos de cancelación?	What are the cancellation costs?
¿Cuántas estrellas tiene el hotel?	How many stars does the hotel have?
¿Cuánto cuesta la habitación por noche?	How much does the room cost per night?
¿Dispone el hotel de un gimnasio?	Does the hotel have a gym?
¿Disponen de un servicio de autobús desde el aeropuerto?	Does the hotel have an airport shuttle service?
¿Está el hotel adaptado para minusválidos?	Is your hotel handicapped accessible?
¿Están permitidas las mascotas?	Are pets allowed?

¿Hasta cuándo se podría cancelar sin coste alguno?	Until when can you cancel free of charge?
¿Ofrecen servicio de alquiler de bicicletas?	Do you offer a bicycle rental service?
¿Tienen aire acondicionado o ventilador las habitaciones?	Do the rooms have air conditioning or fan?
¿Tiene aparcamiento dentro del recinto del hotel?	Do you have parking spaces within the hotel area?
¿Tiene sauna?	Do you have a sauna?
¿Tienen caja fuerte?	Do you have safes?
¿Tienen calefacción las habitaciones?	Do you have heating in the rooms?
¿Tienen cocina?	Do you have a kitchen?
¿Tienen Wifi?	Is WiFi included in your hotel?
albergue juvenil	Youth Hostel
apartamento (de vacaciones)	holiday flat
bungaló	Bungalow
camping	Campsite
casa rural	cottage
Estoy buscando un hotel en el centro.	I'm looking for a hotel in the city centre/downtown.
hostal	Hostel
motel	Motel
parador	Service area
posada, pensión	Pension

Booking

¿Cómo puedo llegar al hotel en transporte público?	How can I reach the hotel by public transport?
¿Cuál es su número de teléfono?	What is your telephone number?
¿Cuántas noches quiere reservar?	How many nights do you want to book?
¿Debo pagar por adelantado o en el alojamiento?	Do I have to pay in advance or in the hotel?
¿Me puede dar la información de su tarjeta de crédito para completar la reserva?	Could you please give me the credit card details to complete your booking?
¿Podría deletrear su nombre y apellido, por favor?	Can you please spell your first and last names?
¿Tengo que pagar en el check-in o en el check-out?	Do I have to pay at check-in or check-out?
¿Tienen habitaciones libres?	Do you have rooms available?
Llegaré sobre las … horas a su hotel.	I will arrive at your hotel at around…
Querría una habitación familiar.	I would like a family room.
Quiero reservar una habitación doble.	I want to book a double room.
Quiero una habitación de (no) fumadores.	I want a (non-)smoking room.
Quiero una habitación individual.	I want a single room.

Check-in

¿A qué hora es el desayuno?	What time is breakfast served?
¿Dónde está el ascensor?	Where is the lift/elevator?
¿Hay lavandería aquí?	Do you have a laundry room?

¿Me puede poner el despertador a las ... horas?	Could you set my alarm for me at...
Cuarto de baño privado	Private bathroom
garaje subterráneo	underground car park
Hacer el check-in	check in
Huésped	Guest
La habitación dispone de minibar.	The room has a mini bar.
Llave de la habitación	Room key
Media pensión	Half board
Pagar con tarjeta	Pay with debit card
Pago en efectivo	Cash payment
Pensión completa	Full board
Piscina	Swimming pool
Planta	floor
planta baja	ground floor
primera planta	1st floor
Recepción	Reception
Recepcionista	Receptionist
Sábanas/ropa de cama	Bed linen
Servicio de habitaciones	room service
Sótano	Basement

Complaints

¿Me puede dar otra manta?	Could you give me another blanket?
Es demasiado ruidoso.	It's too loud.
No funciona el aire acondicionado.	The air conditioning's broken.
No funciona la calefacción.	The heater doesn't work.
No sale agua caliente.	There's no hot water.
Queja	complaint

Check-out

¿A qué hora tenemos que dejar la habitación?	What time do we have to check out?
¿Podemos dejar nuestras maletas en el cuarto de almacenamiento?	May we leave our bags in the luggage compartment?
¿Me puede devolver mi fianza, por favor?	Can you please return my security deposit?

Camping

¿Dónde está el baño?	Where is the toilet?
¿Dónde puedo tirar la basura?	Where can I dispose of the garbage?
apagar la hoguera	put out the fire
camping	campsite
camping gas/hornillo	camping gas cooker
caravana	motorhome, RV
cerilla	match
esterilla	mat
hacer una hoguera/lumbre	light the fire
hamaca	hammock
hoguera	fire
linterna	flashlight
mazo	mallet
mechero	lighter
mesa plegable	folding table
Necesitamos electricidad, por favor.	We need power, please.
prismáticos	binoculars
repelente, antimosquitos	insect protection
saco de dormir	sleeping bag
sillas plegables	folding chairs
tienda de campaña	tent
toldo	sunroof

BBQ time!
(more details on eating and drinking at level 4)

¿Se puede hacer barbacoa?	Is it legal to barbecue here?
cubiertos de plástico *(Pl.)*	Plastic cutlery
nevera portátil	Cool box
parrilla, barbacoa	Grill place
pastillas encendedoras	Grill lighter
pincho/pinchito	Skewer
pinzas para barbacoa	Grill tongs
platos de plástico *(Pl.)*	Plastic plate
tazas *(Pl.)*	cup, mug
Termo	Thermos flask
vasos de plástico *(Pl.)*	Plastic mugs

Holiday apartment

armario	cupboard/closet
balcón	balcony
bañera	bathtub
cafetera	coffee maker
calentador de agua	kettle
Cama	bed
cama plegable	folding bed
canales de pago	pay-per-view channels
Cocina	kitchen
cocina de gas	gas stove
congelador	freezer
cuarto de baño	bathroom
ducha	shower
enchufe	socket
frigorífico	fridge
horno	oven
juegos de mesa	board games
lavadora	washing machine

mesa	dining table
microondas	microwave
papel higiénico	toilet paper
patio	yard
placa eléctrica, vitro	stove
plancha	iron
productos de limpieza	detergents
secador (de pelo)	hairdryer
secadora	tumble dryer
sofá	sofa
sofá cama	sofa bed
tabla de planchar	ironing board
taburete	stool, high chair
televisor, televisión	television
tendedero	laundry rack
terraza	terrace
tostadora	toaster

Exercises & games

1. Match the pairs of words which have a relation (so same category). Several combinations are possible.

e.g. Aire acondicionado ←→ Hotel
   Aire acondicionado ←→ Apartamento

(because air conditioning is normally available both in the hotel and in an apartment)

microondas	lavandería	Sauna	sábanas
camping	enchufe	apartamento	mesa
caja fuerte	barbacoa	tostadora	calefacción
prismáticos	hotel	Cocina	televisor
habitación doble	gimnasio	saco de dormir	piscina

2. Fill in the gaps. For each pair of words either the word in Spanish or the one in English is missing:

recepción   ______________________________

servicio de habitaciones   ______________________________

double bed   ______________________________

shower   ______________________________

bañera   ______________________________

fire   ______________________________

planta baja   ______________________________

room key   ______________________________

cool box   ______________________________

hornillo   ______________________________

Level 4
Eating & drinking

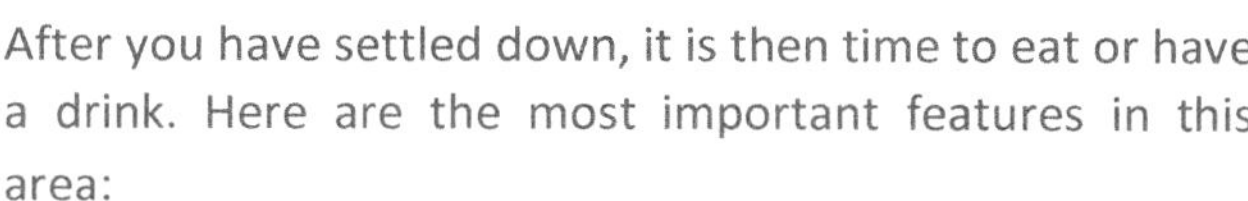

After you have settled down, it is then time to eat or have a drink. Here are the most important features in this area:

Top phrases

¿Me puede traer el menú?	Could you bring me the menu?
¿Sirven tapas aquí?	Do you serve tapas here?
Una mesa para dos, por favor.	A table for two, please.
Quiero una cerveza bien fría, por favor.	I'd like a cold beer, please.
La cuenta, por favor.	Could I have the bill/check, please?

Meals

Tip: In Spain we have different habits regarding meal times. Lunch is usually taken between 2 and 3 pm, dinner between 9 and 10 pm. Be aware of this when you visit Spain...

desayuno	breakfast
aperitivo	Aperitif
piscolabis, tentempié	Bite
comida, almuerzo	Lunch
merienda	afternoon snack
cena	dinner/supper
comer	to eat
beber	to drink
tapear	to eat tapas

Restaurants

¿Cuánto tiempo tenemos que esperar?	How much longer do we have to wait? *(in case you sign up for the waiting list at a full restaurant)*
¿Está la cocina abierta todavía?	Are you still serving food? *(in case you arrived too late at the restaurant)*
¿Me puede recomendar un restaurante barato?	Could you recommend a cheap restaurant?
¿Me puede recomendar un restaurante bueno?	Could you recommend a good restaurant?
¿Me puede recomendar un restaurante cercano?	Could you recommend a restaurant nearby?
¿Sirven comida local/típica aquí?	Is local food served here?
¿Tienen buffet libre?	Do you have an all-you-can-eat buffet?
¿Tienen comida vegana?	Do you have vegan food?
¿Tienen comida vegetariana?	Do you have vegetarian food?
¿Tienen terraza?	Do you have a terrace?
Asador	Steakhouse
bar de pintxos[9]	pintxos bar
Busco un (restaurante) asiático en esta zona.	I'm looking for an Asian restaurant in the area.
mesón	Restaurant
Querría reservar una mesa para dos a las 15 horas.	I'd like to book a table for two at 3:00.
restaurante africano	African restaurant
restaurante argentino	Argentinian restaurant
restaurante asiático	Asian restaurant
restaurante de comida rápida	fast food restaurant

---

[9] Pintxos is written "pinchos" in Spanish. The writing with "tx" instead of "ch" is common in Basque. These tapas bars are very popular in the Basque Country, in the rest of Spain they are called "bar de tapas".

restaurante español	Spanish restaurant
restaurante griego	Greek restaurant
restaurante italiano	Italian restaurant
restaurante mexicano	Mexican restaurant
snack bar, cafetería	Snack bar
Taberna	Tavern
Tasca	Pub

Orders

¡Que aproveche!	Enjoy your meal!
¿Cuál es el plato típico aquí?	What is the local dish here?
¿Cuál es la especialidad de la casa?	What's the specialty of the house?
¿Desean pedir algo más?	Anything else?
¿Lleva el plato alguna guarnición?	Is this dish served with a side dish?
¿Podemos pagar por separado?	May we pay separately?
¿Qué desean comer?	What do you want to eat?
¿Qué nos recomienda?	What do you recommend?
¿Todo junto o separado?	Together or separately?
Camarero	Waiter
Disculpe, esto no lo hemos pedido.	Sorry, we didn't order that.
Factura	Receipt
Mi comida está fría, ¿la puede recalentar?	My food is already cold, could you warm it up?
Propina	Tip
Se ha roto mi vaso, ¿me puede traer otro?	My glass is broken, could you bring me another one?
Sólo vamos a tomar algo.	We're just going for a drink.
Todo muy rico, gracias.	Everything was delicious, thanks.

For allergic people

Soy alérgico/ **Tengo alergia al/a la...**	I am allergic to…
altramuces	lupines
apio	celery
cacahuetes	peanuts
crustáceos	crustaceans
frutos secos	dried fruit
gluten	gluten
huevos	eggs
lactosa	lactose
marisco	seafood
mostaza	mustard
pescado	fish
sésamo	sesame
soja	soya
sulfito	sulphite

Common vocabulary

carta de bebidas	list of beverages
carta de postres	dessert menu
carta de vinos	wine list
copa de vino	wine glass
cuchara	spoon
cucharilla	teaspoon
cuchillo	knive
entrantes, entremeses	appetizers, starters
menú del día	daily menu
plato	plate, dish
plato principal	main course
postre	dessert
primer plato	first course
segundo plato	main course

servilleta	napkin
tenedor	fork
vaso	glass

Most common food and dishes
(even more at Level 6 > At the supermarket)

Beverages

agua con gas	sparkling mineral water
agua del grifo	tap water
agua mineral	still water
cava	champagne
cerveza	beer
limonada	lemonade
mosto	grape juice
oporto	Port wine
refrescos	non-alcoholic beverages
rosé	rosé
sidra	northern Spanish cider
vino	wine
vino blanco	white wine
vino espumoso	champagne
vino tinto	red wine
zumo de manzana	apple juice
zumo de naranja	orange juice
zumo de piña	pineapple juice

Starters

aceite	oil
aceite de oliva	olive oil
aceitunas	olives

ajo blanco	southern Spanish cold soup made from garlic, bread and almonds
… al ajillo	with garlic
aliño	salad dressing
bocadillo de calamares	squid sandwich
calamares	squid rings
calamares a la romana	breaded squid rings
champiñones	mushrooms
croquetas	croquettes
empanadas	filled dough pies (large)
empanadillas	filled dough pies (small)
ensalada	salad
ensalada mixta	mixed salad
gazpacho	Spanish cold tomato soup
huevo frito	fried egg
huevos revueltos	scrambled eggs
jamón ibérico	Iberico ham
jamón serrano	serrano ham
mojo picón	spicy dip from the Canary Islands
patatas bravas	seasoned fries (with spicy sauce on top)
patatas fritas	French fries
pimienta	pepper
pimientos de Padrón	chilies
pisto manchego	Spanish vegetable dish, usually served with a fried egg
queso	cheese
queso de cabra	goat cheese
queso de oveja	sheep's cheese
sal	Salt
salmorejo	Spanish cold tomato soup (with toasted bread, oil, garlic, eggs and ham)

sopa	soup
sopa de fideos	noodle soup
tortilla	omelette
vinagre	vinegar

Main course

Pasta

canelones	cannelloni
espaguetis	spaghetti
lasaña	lasagna
macarrones	macaroni
pasta	pasta
pizza	pizza

Vegetables

alcachofas	artichokes
berenjenas	aubergines, eggplants
calabacines	courgette, zucchini
espárragos	asparagus
espinacas	spinach
garbanzos	chickpeas
judías blancas	white beans
judías verdes	green beans
lentejas	lentils
patatas	potatoes
verdura	vegetables

Stews

| **caldo gallego** | Spanish stew with vegetables and beans |

cocido madrileño	Spanish stew: noodle soup with chickpeas, meat (chicken, blood sausage, chorizo), potatoes and carrots
cocido montañés	Bean soup from Cantabria (Spain)
fabada	Bean soup from Asturias (Spain)
ropa vieja	braised beef with vegetables (typical from Cuba and Spain)

Meat

albóndigas	meatballs
beicon, panceta	bacon
carne	meat
carne de cerdo	pork
carne de cordero	lamb meat
carne de ternera	beef
chuletón	steak
entrecot	entrecôte
filete	steak
filete empanado	breaded steak
filete ruso	hamburger steak
hamburguesa	burger
morcilla	blood sausage
pavo	turkey
pechuga de pollo	chicken breast
pinchito moruno	brochette
pollo	chicken
salchichas	sausages
secreto ibérico	juicy cut of Iberico pork
solomillo	sirloin

Rice

arroz	rice

arroz a banda	Rice dish from eastern Spain
arroz a la cubana	Rice dish with white rice, fried egg and tomato sauce
arroz negro	Rice dish with squid and its ink
paella	Spanish rice dish (various kinds: with vegetables, chicken meat, beans, seafood...)

Fish and seafood

anchoas	anchovies
arenque	herring
atún	tuna
bacalao	cod
boquerones	fried anchovies
camarones	shrimps
ceviche	raw fish in lemon juice
chipirones[10]	small squid rings
dorada	sea bream
gambas	prawns
langosta	lobster
langostinos	large shrimps
lenguado	sole
lubina	sea bass
marisco	seafood
merluza	hake
panga	pangasius
pescado	fish
pez espada	swordfish
pulpo	octopus
salmón	salmon

---

[10] Also known as "puntillitas" or "chopitos"

Desserts

arroz de leche	rice pudding
crema catalana	Spanish version of *crème brûlée*
flan	caramel pudding
fresas con nata	sweetened strawberries with whipped cream
fruta	fruit
macedonia	fruit salad
melocotón en almíbar	pieces of peach in own juice
melón	melon
mousse de chocolate	chocolate mousse
mousse de limón	lemon mousse
natillas	custard
piña en almíbar	pineapple rings in own juice
plátano	banana
polvito uruguayo	(*Uruguay, Canary Islands*) Dessert with caramel topping, biscuits, butter, milk, cream
sandía	watermelon
strudel de manzana	apple strudel
tarta de queso	cheesecake
tocino de cielo	pudding with egg yolk, sugar and water
yogur	yoghurt

In the bar

¡Chin chin!	Cheers! *(whenever we toast with champagne)*
¡Salud!	Cheers!
¿Qué te pido?	What shall I order for you?
aguardiante	Liquor
bebidas espirituosas	spirituous beverages
caña	beer bottle
cerveza de barril	draught beer
champán	champagne

clara	*Radler* (beer mixed with sparkling lemonade)
Esta ronda la pago yo.	This round is on me.
jarra (de cerveza)	Beer mug
jerez	Sherry
Me tomaré...	I'll take...
Otra ronda, por favor.	Another round, please.
sangría	sangria

At the coffee shop[11]

Kinds of coffee

(café) cortado	Coffee with a little frothed milk
(café) manchado	Espresso with lots of milk foam
barraquito	*(Tenerife)* Coffee served with four layers: coffee, condensed milk, Spanish liquor and milk foam

café	coffee
café americano	Americano coffee
café bombón	Coffee with condensed milk
café con hielo	iced coffee (served with a glass of ice cubes, the coffee is drunk ice-cold)
café con leche	Latte (coffee with milk)
café solo	Black coffee
capuchino	Cappuccino
carajillo	espresso served with brandy or whisky
descafeinado de máquina	decaf coffee (from the coffee machine)
descafeinado de sobre	Decaf instant coffee (from a packet)
espresso	espresso

[11] Or coffee bar. Nothing to do with the Dutch coffee shops :)

Kinds of tea

manzanilla	chamomile tee
mate	mate *(very popular South American green tea)*
menta poleo	peppermint tea
rooibos	fruit tea
té	tea
té blanco	white tea
té con limón	tea with lemon
té frío	ice tea
té negro	black tea
té rojo	red tea
té verde	green tea
tila	linden blossom tea

Cakes

bamba	Cream puff
berlina	Doughnut with a jam filling
cruasán	Croissant
donut	Doughnut
ensaimada	*(Mallorca)* sweetened pastry with a spiral shape
galletas	Cookies, biscuits
magdalena	muffin
merengue	meringe
napolitana	Puff pastry bag filled with chocolate
pastel	Cake
quesadilla	*(northern Spain)* Cheesecake
tarta	Cake
torrijas	fried slices of bread dipped in milk and beaten eggs

Other drinks

batido	Milkshake
batido de chocolate	Chocolate milkshake

Exercises & games

1. This time I suggest you a role play. Find a partner and take on the roles of waiter and customer in a bar and/or restaurant. Scroll through the vocabulary and standard phrases for the respective roles and simulate a small talk. By not only reading but also actively practicing these new skills, you will find that you can learn it faster with the purpose of being able to defend yourself later on when you order. Ideally, you swap roles and have a second conversation.

2. The Cookie Monster was so hungry today that he devoured letters from the words below. Could you possibly add the missing letters to the words? (area: food or drink). Hint: next to the word, we indicate how many letters are missing in total.

e.g.: 0. CA__E (2) → CA**RN**E

1.	J__ÓN (2)	11.	_AB_D_ (3)
2.	SA__ÓN (2)	12.	TO_TI__A (3)
3.	V__O (2)	13.	CE__EZ_ (3)
4.	_ERE_ (2)	14.	GA__E_AS (3)
5.	JA__A (2)	15.	B_T_D_ (3)
6.	P_Á_ANO (2)	16.	S_L__IC_AS (4)
7.	BA___AO (3)	17.	_SPI___AS (4)
8.	_AN__ÍA (3)	18.	T_RT_ DE Q__SO (4)
9.	P_E__A (3)	19.	__ZPA__O (4)
10.	SO_OMI__O (3)	20.	C_F_ CON LE___ (5)

Level 5

City, mountain or beach?

8

After you have already put down the luggage and feel already full, it is time for a city tour. Or maybe you go for a trip into the nature or a hike. Or you just want to relax on the beach under the parasol. You will find everything in this level.

City

Top phrases

¿Me puede dar un mapa de la ciudad, por favor?	Could you give me a city map, please?
¿Nos puede hacer una foto, por favor?	Could you take a photo for us?
¿Ofrecen descuentos para grupos/ancianos/niños/estudiantes?	Do you have discounts for groups/older people/children/students?
¿Se pueden hacer fotos con flash?	Is it permitted to take photos with flash?
Busco la oficina de turismo.	I am looking for the tourist information.
Hola, estoy buscando la catedral, ¿me puede decir cómo llegar?	Hello, I am looking for the cathedral, can you tell me how to get there?
Me he perdido.	I am lost.

Places of interest

alameda	Avenue
arco, puerta	Gate
ayuntamiento	City hall
basílica	Basilica

biblioteca	Library
calle	Street
castillo	Castle
catedral	Cathedral
estatua	Statue
galería de arte	Art Gallery
iglesia	Church
jardín	Garden
mezquita	Mosque
monumento	Sightseeing, monument
muralla	Wall
museo	Museum
museo arqueológico	archaeological museum
museo de arte	art-history museum
museo de ciencias	Science Museum
museo de ciencias naturales	Museum of Natural History
museo de historia	history museum
obelisco	Obelisk
palacio	palace, castle
parque	Park
paseo	Promenade
plaza	Square
puente	Bridge
rascacielos	Skyscrapers
ruinas	Ruins
sinagoga	Synagogue
teatro	Theatre
templo	Temple
torre de televisión	TV tower
torre del reloj	Clock tower
universidad	University

Museums & art galleries

¿Cuánto cuesta la entrada?	How much is the ticket?
¿Hay alguna exposición temporal?	Is there any temporary exhibition at the moment?
alfarero	Potter
arte	art
artista	artists
cerámica	Ceramics
cuadro	Picture
dibujante	Draftsman
dibujo	drawing
donación	Donation
donar	donate
entrada gratuita	free entry
escultor	sculptor
escultura	sculpture
gratis, gratuito	free of charge
guardarropas	cloakroom
impresión	print
marco	picture frame
obra maestra	Masterpiece
pintor	Painter
pintura	Paintings
Por favor, no tocar.	Please do not touch.
retrato	Portrait
talla en madera	Woodwork

Art movements

Arte clásico	classical art
Arte moderno	modern art
Barroco	Baroque
Cubismo	Cubism

Expresionismo	Expressionism
Gótico	Gothic
Impresionismo	Impressionism
Renacimiento	Renaissance
Románico	Romanesque

Tours

¿Cuándo empieza el siguiente tour?	When does the next city tour start?
¿Cuánto dura el tour?	How long does the city tour last?
¿Qué incluye el tour?	What is included in the tour?
¿Tienen audioguías en inglés?	Do you have audio guides in English?

Bus turístico	Hop on hop off bus
Disponibilidad	Availability
Excursión al campo	Land excursion
Excursión de un día	Day trip
Guía turístico	travel guide
Parada	Stop
Tour en barco	Boat tour
Tour en bicicleta	Bicycle tour
Tour gratuito, free tour	free city tour *(the tourists usually pay a tip)*

Travelling with...

Elderly people

¡Socorro, ayuda!	Help!
Balneario	Health resort
baños termales	Thermal bath
crucero	Cruise
gente mayor	older persons

golpe de calor	Heat stroke
Llame a un doctor.	Call a doctor.
medicamentos	Drugs, medicines
spa	Spa

Handicapped

accesible	barrier-free
adaptado a sillas de ruedas	wheelchair accessible
ascensor	elevator, lift
asistencia a discapacitados	assistance for the disabled
baños para discapacitados	Disabled toilet
discapacitados, minusválidos	Disabled
perro guía	Guide dog
rampas de acceso	Access ramp
servicio de silla de ruedas	Wheelchair service
teléfono de emergencia	emergency phone number

Kids

bosque multiaventura	Outdoor climbing forest
finca	farm
parque acuático	Water park
parque de atracciones	Theme park
parque infantil	playground
piscina para niños	Children's swimming pool
zoo	Zoo

Beach or mountain?

There are two types of holidaymakers: mountain people and beach people. For all of them, there is definitely something here for the desired holiday.

The weather

¿Qué tiempo hace hoy?	What is the weather like today?
Aguanieve	Sleet
Anticiclón	High pressure area, anticyclones
Borrasca	low pressure area
Calor	Heat
Está lloviendo.	It's raining.
Está nevando.	It's snowing.
Estamos a …. grados.	It's… degrees.
Frío	Cold
Granizo	Hail
Hace calor.	It's hot.
Hace frío.	It's cold.
Hace viento.	It's windy.
Helada	Frost
Humedad	Humidity
inundación/riada	Flood
Lluvia	Rain
Niebla	Fog
Nieve	Snow
Nubes	Clouds
nublado	cloudy
Precipitaciones	Precipitation
presión atmosférica	Air pressure
previsión del tiempo	weather forecast
sol	Sun

soleado	sunny
temperatura	Temperature
Tengo calor.	It's hot to me.
Tengo frío.	I'm cold.
tormenta	Storm
tornado	Tornado
tsunami	Tsunami
viento	Wind

For mountain lovers

abrigo	Hiking jacket
altura	Height
arnés	Climbing harness
Bastones de senderismo	Hiking poles
botas de montaña	Hiking boots
botiquín (de primeros auxilios)	First aid kit
bragas	knickers, panties
brújula	Compass
bufanda	Scarf
calcetines	Socks
calzoncillos	Underpants
camiseta de manga larga	Long sleeve shirt
camiseta interior	Undershirt
camiseta transpirable	sweaty T-shirt
cima	Summit
crampones	Crampons
cuerda	Rope
empinado	Steep
esquí	Skiing
esquiar	To ski
Etapa	stage
Frontal	Headlamp
gorro de montaña	Mountain cap

GPS	Navigator
Guantes	Gloves
hacer senderismo	To hike
Hemos planeado una ruta de 20 kilómetros.	We have planned a 20-kilometer route.

ir cuesta abajo	To go downhill
ir cuesta arriba	To go uphill
Llano	Flat
Mapa	(Country) map
Mochila	backpack
Montaña	Mountain
navaja suiza	Swiss knife
Paisaje	Landscape
pantalón impermeable	waterproof hiking pants
pantalones cortos	(hiking) shorts
pañuelo	bandana
pico	Top
piolet	Ice pick

polar	Fleece jacket
ropa	Clothing
saco de dormir	sleeping bag
senderismo	Trekking
senderista	Hiker
sudadera	Sweater
sujetador	bra
telesilla	Cable car
walkie-talkie[12]	walkie-talkie

For beach lovers

arena	sand
bañador	swimming trunks
bikini	bikini
bronceado	tanning
broncearse	get a tan
castillo de arena	sandcastle
chanclas	flip-flops
chiringuito	beach bar
cometa	kite
costa	coast
cubo	bucket
flotador	floating ring
frisbi, plato volador	frisbee
gafas de sol	sunglasses
Helado	ice-cream
Hielo	ice cube
Lago	lake
Lancha	motorboat
Mar	sea
marea alta	high tide
marea baja	low tide

---

[12] pronounced /'walki 'talki/

Mareas	tides
Nudismo	nudism
Océano	ocean
Olas	waves
Orilla	shore
Pareo	large scarf worn by women on the beach (kind of a dress)

paseo marítimo	promenade
pelota de playa	beach ball
playa	beach
playa nudista	nudist beach
polo	icy pop
protector solar	sunblock
quemadura	sunburn
resaca	undercurrent
socorrista	lifeguard
sombrilla	beach umbrella
submarinismo, buceo	scuba diving
tabla de surf	surfboard
toalla	towel
tumbona	deckchair

Exercises & games

1. Fill in the gaps:

Van Gogh es un ________ [*painter* or *artist*] del arte impresionista *(impressionist)*.

La entrada al ______ [*museum*] no es ________ [*free of charge*].

No tengo ganas de andar, vamos a tomar un ____________ [*hop on hop off bus*].

Los niños quieren ir a ver animales, así que iremos al ___.

Yo visitaré la ______ [*Square*] Mayor en Madrid.

España es conocida por sus grandes _________. [*Castles*].

La Alhambra de Granada es un ________ [*palace*] árabe.

¡Vamos a la ________, oh, oh, oh! *(Lyrics of a famous song from the 80s)*.

Me encanta la _________ [*mountain*], pero ahora en invierno hace mucho ______ [*cold*].

Creo que ____________ [*rain*], veo muchas ________ [*clouds*] negras.

En verano me gusta comer ________ [*ice-cream*] en los ___________ [*beach bars*] de Mallorca.

Mi hijo ha construido un __________________ [*sandcastle*]. Voy a hacer una foto.

Vocabulary	
me encanta	I love
(yo) creo	I think
(yo) veo	I see
me gusta...	I like
Hijo	Son
Construido	Built
no tener ganas de...	Not fancy
Tomar	(*in this context*) take public transportation
Animales	animals
así que	so, therefore

2. Complete the crossword puzzle with the words of this level from the categories Weather, Mountain and Beach (number 3 consists of three words, the blank spaces are removed here):

Horizontales *(across)*

1 backpack
2 fleece jacket
3 sleeping bag
4 cold
5 undercurrent
6 beach
7 clouds
8 sun
9 sea
10 flat
11 wind
12 landscape
13 flip-flops

Verticales *(down)*

14 headlamp
15 heat
16 ice cream
17 sand
18 tides
19 tanning
20 hiker

(crossword puzzle on the next page)

Level 6
Going shopping

9

Enough sightseeing? You will find the most important stuff about shopping at this level.

At the mall

¿Le puedo ayudar?	May I help you?
agencia de viajes	travel agency
Centro comercial	department store, mall
Cine	Cinema
de rebajas	On clearance sale
Droguería	Drugstore
Ir de compras	go shopping
Joyería	Jewellery shop
Lavandería	Laundry
Librería	Bookstore
liquidación por fin de temporada	Season sale
Menaje	Household contents
menaje de cocina	Kitchen utensils
Negocio	business
Óptica	Optics
Papelería	Stationery
Peluquería	Hairdressing salon
sala de juegos, recreativos	gambling house
Servicio de atención al cliente	customer service
Sólo estoy mirando.	I just want to look/see.
Tienda	Store
Tienda de muebles	Furniture store
Tintorería	Dry cleaner

Clothing shop

¿Cuál es el plazo de cambio?	What is the exchange period?
¿Cuál es el plazo de devolución?	What is the return period?
¿Dónde están los probadores?	Where are the changing rooms?
¿Me lo puede envolver para regalo?	Could you gift-wrap it for me?
¿Me lo puedo probar?	Can I try it on?
¿Me puede dar una bolsa?	Could you give me a bag?
¿Tiene esta prenda en verde?	Do you have this garment in green?
¿Tiene una talla más grande?	Do you have a larger size?
¿Tiene una talla más pequeña?	Do you have a smaller size?
El vestido me hace delgada.	This dress makes me look slim.
El vestido me hace gorda.	The dress makes me fat.
Esta prenda está defectuosa. ¿Tiene otra quizás?	This garment is defective. Do you have another one?
Le queda bien.	It looks good on you.
Los pijamas están de oferta.	The pyjamas are on sale.
No aceptamos devoluciones, sólo cambios.	We don't accept returns, only exchanges.
No me queda bien.	It doesn't fit me well.
Querría descambiar esta falda, por favor.	I'd like to exchange this skirt, please.
Querría devolver esta camiseta, por favor.	I'd like to return this T-shirt, please.
Sí, claro.	Yes, of course.
Te queda perfecto.	It fits you like a glove.
Tengo/uso la (talla) XS/S/M/L /XL.	I use the size XS/S/M/L/XL.
abrigo	Coat
americana, chaqueta	Jacket
blusa	Blouse
botas	boots
camisa	Shirt
chaleco	vest

cinturón	Belt
corbata	Tie
falda	Rock
gorra	Cap
jersey	Sweaters
katiuskas, botas de goma	rubber boots
lencería	Lingerie
medias	Stockings
pajarita	bow tie
pantalones	Pants
pijama	Pajamas
ropa	Clothing
ropa de caballero	menswear
ropa de señora	ladies' fashion
sombrero	Hat
tacón	heel
tienda de ropa	Clothing store
traje	Suit
vestido	dress
zapatillas	sneakers
zapatos	shoes

Bookshop

¿Se pueden hojear los libros?	Are we allowed to flip through the books?
cuadernillo	Workbook
cuaderno	Block
diccionario	Dictionary
Estoy buscando un bestseller. ¿Qué libro me recomienda?	I'm looking for a bestseller. Which book do you recommend?
guía de viajes	Travel book
libro	Book
libro de autoayuda	Self help book

libro de bolsillo	Paperback
libro de cocina	Cookbook
libro de idiomas	Language book
libro de pasatiempos	puzzle book
libro de texto	Textbook
novela	novel
periódico	newspaper
revista	Magazine

At the consumer electronics retailer

accesorios	Accessories
adaptador de viaje universal	Travel adapters
alargador	Extension cable
altavoces	Speaker
asistente de voz	Voice assistant
auriculares	Headphones
batería externa	Powerbank
cámara de fotos	Photo camera
comedias	Comedy
disco de música	Audio CD
documental	Documentary
dron	Drone
electrodomésticos	Large household appliances
escáner	Scanner
impresora	Printer
monitor	Monitor
móvil	Mobile phone, cellphone
smartphone	smartphone
no recomendada para menores de 18 años	NC-18, R18, BBFC 18
película de acción	Action movie
película de ciencia ficción	Science fiction movie

película policíaca	Thriller
películas	Films
películas eróticas	Erotic movies
películas infantiles	Films for children
pilas	Batteries
portátil	laptop, notebook
pre-escuchar (un cd)	Pre-listening (a CD)
reproductor de dvd	DVD player
series de televisión	TV series
tablet	Tablet
(disco de) vinilo	Vinyl record

Souvenir shop

abanico	fan
chapa	badge
dedal	thimble
imán	magnet
llavero	keychain
miniatura	miniature
pin	pin
placas	plates
posavasos	coaster
postal	postcard
sello	stamp
souvenir, recuerdo	souvenir

At the market

¿A qué hora abren el mercado?	What time does the market open?
¿Cuánto pesa?	How heavy is that?
¿Dónde puedo comprar productos locales?	Where can I buy local products?
¿Hasta qué hora está abierto el mercado?	Until when does the market remain open?
¿Necesita el ticket?	Do you need the receipt?
Charcutería	butcher' s shop
Flores	Flowers
Floristería	Flower shop
Frutería	Fruit shop
Mercado	Market
Mercado de abastos	Wholesale Market
Panadería	Bakery
Pastelería	Confectionery
Pescadería	Fish market
Póngame un kilo de naranjas, por favor.	I want a kilo of oranges, please.
ramo de flores	Bouquet
Tetería	Tea house

At the flea market

¿Me lo puede dejar más barato?	Could you lower the price?
¿Por cuánto vende este artículo?	What is your price proposal for this product?
Le doy/ofrezco…	I'll give you… (*+amount of money*)
Lo siento, es demasiado caro.	Sorry, it's too expensive for me.
Me lo tengo que pensar.	I'll have to think it over.
Mercadillo, rastro	flea market
Vale, me lo llevo.	All right, I'll take it.

At the supermarket

Caja	Cash counter
Cajero	Cashier
Carrito de la compra	Shopping Cart
Cinta	Conveyor belt

For meat lovers

cangrejo	Crab
carne picada	minced meat
chorizo	Spanish seasoned sausage
chuleta	cutlet
conejo	Rabbit
conservas	canned food
costillas	ribs
filete de cadera	Rump steak
ganso, oca	Goose
mejillones	Mussels
muslo de pollo	Chicken leg
pato	Duck
salami	Salami
salchichón	Hot pepperoni sausage
sardinas	Sardines
trucha	Trout

For veggies

leche	Milk
leche desnatada	Skimmed milk
leche entera	Whole milk
leche semidesnatada	Semi-skimmed milk
manteca	lard
mantequilla	Butter
miel	honey

nata	Cream
nata amarga	Sour cream
queso azul	Blue cheese
queso cremoso	Soft cheese
queso curado	Hard cheese
queso manchego	Manchego cheese

For vegans

aguacate	avocado
ajo	garlic
albaricoque	apricot
almendras	almonds
arroz integral	whole grain rice
bambú	bamboo
brócoli	broccoli
castañas	chestnuts
cebolla	onion
cebollino	chives
cereales	cereals
cereza	cherry
chirimoya	cherimoya
ciruela	plum
coco	coconut
col de Bruselas	Brussels sprout
coliflor	cauliflower
copos de avena	oats
frambuesa	raspberry
guisantes	peas
hummus	hummus
jengibre	ginger
kiwi	kiwi
lechuga	lettuce
legumbres	vegetables

maíz	corn
mandarina	tangerine
nueces	nuts
pan integral	wholemeal bread
pepino	cucumber
pera	pear
pimiento	pepper
pomelo	grapefruit
puerro	leek
quinoa	quinoa
semillas de chía	chia seeds
tofu	tofu
tomates	tomatoes
uvas	grapes
zanahorias	carrots

Exercises & games

1. Complete the crossword puzzle with the words from this level:

Horizontales

2	newspaper
4	keychain
6	bamboo
7	milk
8	market
10	fish market
12	optics
13	book
15	changing rooms

Verticales

1	vinyl
3	laptop
5	carrots
9	films
11	dress
14	sneakers

2. Find the right word for the descriptions (find the English word and fill in the gaps with the matching Spanish words):

Alcoholic beverage obtained by squeezing grapes: ____________________

Shop where you can buy specifically meat and sausage: ____________________

Shop where you can buy flowers: ____________________

The kind of boots you wear when it rains: ____________________

Device for taking pictures: ____________________

Shop where you can buy tea: ____________________

Street market where you can buy bargains: ____________________

Book in which you can search words in other languages or the meanings of foreign words in your own language: ____________________

Red vegetable often eaten in salads: ____________________

Male piece of clothing that is usually worn at weddings: ____________________

Level 7
Sports and events

10

Not every traveller wants to go to the beach, hike or visit the city. Some simply want to enjoy a football match, go to a concert or experience a bullfight. This is the place for these and other events.

Sport

Football / Soccer

Football is the most popular sport in Spain and South America. The Spanish "La Liga" or the Argentinian "Superliga Argentina" among others are followed all over the world.

aficionados	fans
amistoso	friendly match
árbitro	referee
área grande	penalty area
área pequeña	goal area
asistencia	assist
atacantes, delanteros	strikers
balón	ball
banquillo	bench
camiseta	T-shirt
campeones	champions
campo de fútbol	soccer field
centrocampistas	midfielders
clasificación	standings
club	club
copa	cup
corner, saque de esquina	corner kick
Defensas	defenders
Deporte	sport
Derbi	derby

derbi local	local derby
derrota	defeat
Descanso	break
driblar, regatear	dribble
Empate	tie
entrada fuerte, placaje	tackle
Entrenador	coach
equipo que asciende	promoted team
equipo que desciende	relegated team
Espectadores	spectators
Estadio	stadium
Falta	foul
farolillo rojo	underdog
fuera de juego	offside
fútbol	football, soccer
Futbolista	footballer
Gol	goal
Jornada	matchday
Larguero	crossbar
lateral derecho	right-back
lateral izquierdo	left-back
Líder	leader
Marcar	score
meter gol	score
once inicial	starting lineup
parada	save
partido de preparación	preparation game
partido en casa	home game
partido fuera de casa	away game
Pase	pass
penalti	penalty
pichichi	top scorer
pitar	blow the whistle
portería	goal
portero, arquero	goalkeeper

posesión de balón	ball possession
poste	post
primer tiempo	first half
promoción de ascenso	play-off tournament
prórroga	extra time
rematar de cabeza	heading the ball
saque de banda	throw-in
saque de puerta	goal kick
segundo tiempo	second half
suplentes	substitutes
sustitución	substitution
tarjeta amarilla	yellow card
tarjeta roja	red card
temporada	season
tiempo de descuento	stoppage time
tiro	shot
tiro libre	free kick
Torneo	tournament
traspaso	transfer
trofeo	trophy
victoria	victory

Gym

¿Hay clases de baile?	Are dance lessons offered?
¿Qué actividades hay en este gimnasio?	What sports activities are available in this gym?
abdominales	abs
Barra	Bar
barra de dominadas	Pull-up bar
barra de pesas	barbell
bíceps	biceps
bicicleta elíptica	Cross trainer
bicicleta estática	ergometer
calentamiento	Warm-up

cinta de correr	Treadmill
columna vertebral	Spine
cuádriceps	Quadriceps
discos	weight discs
entrenador personal	fitness trainer
espalda	Back
estirar	stretch
expirar	Breathe out
flexionar	bend
flexiones	push-ups
gemelos	Calves
gimnasio	gym
hacer abdominales	do sit-ups
inspirar	Breathe in
levantamiento de pesas	Strength Training
levantar	lift, pull up
mancuernas	Dumbbells
máquina de remos	Rowing machine
Me quiero apuntar un día.	I want to sign up for a day.
pecho	Breast
piernas	Legs
sauna	Sauna
solarium	Solarium
tríceps	Triceps

Other sports

atletismo	athletics
baloncesto	basketball
balonmano	handball
bolos	bowling
carreras de caballo	horse racing
ciclismo	cycling
equitación	horse riding

escalada	climbing
esquí	skiing
montar en trineo	sledge ride
natación	swimming
patinaje sobre hielo	ice skating
pilates	pilates
ping-pong	table tennis
rocódromo	rockodrome
tenis	tennis
vela	sailing
yoga	yoga

Concerts

bajo	bassist
batería	drummer
canción	song
cantante	singer
concierto	concert
grada	seating row
guitarra	guitar
guitarrista	guitarist
letra de la canción	lyrics
pianista	pianist
piano	piano
recinto	arena
teclado	keyboard
teclista	keyboarder
¡Otra!	Encore!

At the church

Ave maría	Hail Mary
Bautizo	Baptism
Belén, nacimiento	crib

Capilla	chapel
Católico	catholic
Costaleros	bearers
hermandad	brotherhood
Iglesia	Church
Jueves Santo	Maundy Thursday
Matrimonio	marriage
Nazarenos	penitents
Oraciones, rezos	prayers
Padrenuestro	Lord's Prayer
Pascua	Easter
Pasos	floats
Penitencia	penance
Procesiones	processions
Sacerdote	priest
Saeta	Spanish religious song
Viernes Santo	Good Friday

Bullfighting

¡Olé!	exclamation, with which the spectators express their enthusiasm for the bullfight
Banderillas	banderillas (colourful sticks)
Capote	bullfighter's cape
Corridas de toros	bullfights
Estoque	rapier
Hacer el paseíllo	taking a lap around the arena
Lanza	lance
Montera	bullfighter's cap
Picador	picador (bullfighter's assistant)
Plaza de toros	bullring
Tauromaquia	bullfighting
Torero	bullfighter
Toro	bull
Traje de luces	bullfighter's costume

Exercises & games

1. Check out sports websites in Spanish and browse through them. No matter if you don't understand everything, the main idea is that you identify the stuff you have learned in the material and thus assimilate this vocabulary. These are some of the most popular sports websites:

Marca.com	(Spain)
As.com	(Spain)
Olé	(Argentina)
Record	(Mexico)
El Deportivo	(Colombia)
El Bocón	(Peru)

2. Match the pairs of words that have a connection (i.e. the same category). Several combinations are possible.

yoga	plaza de toros	ciclismo	canción
gimnasio	calentamiento	camiseta	centrocampista
poste	piano	abdominales	traje de luces
torero	mancuernas	larguero	guitarrista
portero	sacerdote	concierto	barra de dominadas
iglesia	cantante	tenis	música

Level 8

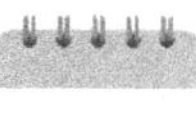

It's party time!

11

Already arrived, much visited and well eaten and drunk? Maybe you already want to relax, celebrate and enjoy a local party. This book has thought about that, here you will find useful tips to communicate with the locals and, if you wish, flirt with them ☺. Attention: the section "flirting" is not quite suitable for kids!

Top phrases

¿A qué hora quedamos esta noche?	What time are we meeting tonight?
¿Dónde hay algún pub irlandés para tomar una cerveza?	Where's an Irish pub for a beer?
¿Dónde hay una buena discoteca?	Where's a good disco?
¿Dónde nos vemos?	Where shall we meet?
¿Hay locales de ambiente en la ciudad?	Are there any gay bars in town?
¿Qué fiesta hay esta noche?	Which party is happening tonight?
¿Qué plan hay esta noche?	What's on tonight?
¿Quieres que te pase a recoger?	You want me to pick you up?
Me apetece bailar salsa.	I feel like salsa.

Meeting new people

¿Cuántos años tienes?	How old are you?
¿De dónde eres?	Where are you from?
¿De qué trabajas?	What do you do for a living?
¿Qué edad tienes?	How old are you?
¿Vives aquí?	Do you live here?
Encantado de conocerte.	Nice to meet you
Me quedo aquí una semana.	I'm staying here a week.

Te presento a mi amigo.	Let me introduce you to my friend.
Trabajo como...	I work as a/an...
profesor *(masc.)*, **profesora** *(fem.)*	teacher
ingeniero, ingeniera	engineer
informático, informática	IT specialist
empresario, empresaria	businessman, businesswoman
psicólogo, psicóloga	psychologist
periodista	journalist
DJ	DJ
abogado, abogada	lawyer, attorney
músico, música	musician
funcionario, funcionaria	public official
policía	policeman, policewoman
granjero, granjera	farmer
autónomo	freelancer
médico	doctor
fisioterapeuta	physiotherapist
dentista	dentist
veterinario	vet
farmacéutico, farmacéutica	pharmacist
peluquero, peluquera	hairdresser
cocinero, cocinera	cook
actor, actriz	actor, actress
Vivo en Inglaterra/Estados Unidos...	I live in the UK/USA...

Flirting

Breaking the ice: pick-up lines

¿Estudias o trabajas?	Do you work or study?
¿Tienes fuego?	Have you got a light?
Hola monada, ¿te puedo invitar a una copa?	Hello cutie, may I invite you for a cocktail?

Romantic

¿Me enseñas el camino a tu corazón?	Will you show me the way to your heart?
Belleza	Beauty
Eres el príncipe/la princesa de mi corazón.	You are the prince/princess of my heart.
Eres un ángel caído del cielo.	You are an angel fallen from heaven.
guapo *(fem.* **guapa***),* **lindo** *(fem.* **linda***)*	handsome/good-looking/beautiful
Me gustaría despertarme cada mañana a tu lado.	I'd like to wake up every morning by your side.
Me haces sonreír.	You make me smile.
Tienes una linda sonrisa.	You have a lovely smile.
Tienes unos ojos preciosos.	You've got beautiful eyes.

Seductive

estar bueno/buena	to be hot
Hacemos buena pareja.	We make a good match.
Hay una química especial entre nosotros dos.	There is this special chemistry between the two of us.
robar un beso	To steal a kiss
rompecorazones	Heartbreaker
seductor	Seducer
Soy muy bueno dando masajes. ¿Quieres que te dé uno?	I am really good at massages. Do you fancy one?

Refusal

¡Largo!	Sod off!
¡Piérdete!	Piss off!, Get lost!
Lo siento, pero no me gustas.	Sorry, but I don't fancy you.
Lo siento, tengo novio/novia.	Sorry, I already have a boyfriend/girlfriend.
Me tengo que ir.	I have to go, I must be off.

Reciprocal interest

¿Te gusto yo?	Do you like me?
Eres muy guapo/guapa.	You're very cute.
Eres muy majo/simpático.	You're very nice/friendly.
Me caes bien.	I like you.
Me gustas.	I fancy you.
Te quiero.	I love you.

The temperature rises...

¡Cómo me pones!	You give me a hard-on!
¡Me pones cachondo!	You turn me on!
¿En tu casa o en la mía?	My place or yours?
¿Vamos a un sitio más íntimo?	Shall we go somewhere more intimate?
Bésame.	Kiss me.
estar cachondo	to be horny

Exercises & games

1. Fill in the gaps with the sentences from the section "Top phrases".

A: Me apetece salir hoy. _______________________.

B: Hay una fiesta latina en la universidad.

A: ¡Genial! _______________________

B: Si quieres podemos ir antes a tomar una cerveza y después bailamos. _______________________

A: Podemos ir al St. Patrick, es muy conocido.

B: Vale. _______________________

A: A las 10. _______________________

B: No, gracias. Iré andando.

2. You're in the disco and made eye contact with him or her. Decide whether or not there is mutual interest in these examples of situations (some with men, some with women):

1) *You:* ¡Hola, guapa! Te invito a una copa.

   Her: No, gracias.   *mutual/not mutual*

2) *You*: Hola, ¿tienes fuego?

   Him: Sí, claro. Toma.

   You: ¿Estudias o trabajas?

   Him: Lo siento, pero no me gustas.   *mutual/not mutual*

3) *You*: Me gusta cómo bailas. ¿Vienes mucho aquí?

   Her: Sí, es mi discoteca preferida. ¿Cómo te llamas?

   You: Mike. Encantado de conocerte. Tienes unos ojos preciosos.

   Her: ¡Gracias! Tú eres muy guapo.   *mutual/not mutual*

4) *You*: Hola, guapo. ¿Estudias o trabajas?

   Him: Soy fisioterapeuta. ¿Y tú?

   You: Yo soy profesor. Me gusta tu trabajo. Me duele la espalda, ¿me puedes dar un masaje?

   Him: Vale, te invito a una copa y después… podemos ir a mi casa y te doy el masaje.

   You: ¡Muy bien, buena idea!   *mutual/not mutual*

Vocabulary

Me duele la espalda.	I have got backache.
Después	later
Buena idea	great idea

Level 9

Latin American Spanish

12

Spanish in Latin America differentiates from Spanish in Spain in the pronunciation, grammar and vocabulary. The South Americans and Spaniards understand each other well, but the earmarks are obvious. The most remarkable features in Latin America are introduced here.

The following abbreviations are attached to words, properties or rules in a specific Latin American country:

All	all	Hon	Honduras
Arg	Argentina	Mex	Mexico
Bol	Bolivia	nic	Nicaragua
Chi	Chile	pan	Panama
Col	Colombia	par	Paraguay
Cos	Costa Rica	per	Peru
Cub	Cuba	pue	Puerto Rico
Dom	Dominican Republic	sal	El Salvador
Ecu	Ecuador	uru	Uruguay
Gua	Guatemala	ven	Venezuela

Pronunciation

These are the most important and obvious differences between Spanish in Spain and South America: 

1. The sound /θ/ in Spain (see Level 1 > Pronunciation > Annotation 12) is pronounced /s/ (*all*).

ceviche /sevitsche/

cerveza   /servesa/

zapato   /sapato/

2. The "r" in a word is not pronounced /r/, but rather replaced by /l/ (*pue, cub, dom*).

amor /aʻmol/

calor /kaʻlol/

azúcar   /aʻsukal/

3. The "y" and "ll" are pronounced /sh/ (*arg, uru*):

EXAMPLES:

pollo /posho/

uruguayo /uruguasho/

yo /sho/

caballo /kabasho/

The intonation of Spanish in Argentina and Uruguay is also very significant, most likely influenced by Italian (due to the immigration of Italians to the region from the 19th century onwards).

Grammar

Some grammatical rules should be highlighted:

1) The subject pronoun of the 2nd person singular (Tú) is used in certain Latin American countries, but "vos" is also common (*par, gua, cos, ecu, sal, hon, col, chi, per, bol, pan*). In Argentina and Uruguay there is no "tú", only "vos".

The verb forms in the 2nd person singular are conjugated differently than with "tú". The final "r" is taken away from the infinitive and replaced by an "s". The verb conjugation is also stressed on the last syllable.

e.g.:

Infinitive	Conjugation with "tú"	Conjugation with "vos"
Salir	tú sales	**vos salís**
Amar	tú amas	**vos amás**
Ser	tú eres	**vos sos** (*irregular*)
Tener	tú tienes	**vos tenés**

2) The subject pronoun of the 2nd person plural (you) is "vosotros" in Spain. However, this pronoun is not used, rather "ustedes" is common there. "Ustedes" is configured like the 3rd person plural. For example:

~~Vosotros sois~~ → ustedes son

~~Vosotros veis~~ → ustedes ven

~~Vosotros escribís~~ → ustedes escriben

~~Vosotros habláis~~ → ustedes hablan

3) The past tenses are simplified. The present perfect does not exist in South America, only in Spain[13]. The present perfect is used in Spain when describing

---

[13] The present perfect is not used either in Spain in Galicia, Asturias or the Canary Islands

an action that has recently been completed. In South America, the past tense is simply used for such actions or others that have recently finished.

<u>Spain</u>

e.g.: Hoy *he desayunado* leche con cacao.

Today I had breakfast with cocoa milk (breakfast finished recently, on the same day).

<u>South America</u>

Hoy **desayuné** leche con cacao.

Vocabulary

There are many words in South America that differ from others in Spain. Within South America you also have the same vocabulary but with different meanings (e.g. "guagua" or "asado").

asado (*arg, chi, cos*)	barbecue
asado (*per, col*)	angry
bencina (*chi*)	petrol/gas
gasofa (*ecu*)	petrol/gas
nafta (*arg*)	petrol/gas
boliche (*bol, arg*)	disco, bar
popote (*mex*)	straw
absorbente (*cub*)	straw
pitillo (*col, ven*)	straw
bombilla[14] (*arg, chi, par, uru, bol*)	metallic straw for mate
boleto (*all*)	ticket
carro (*all*)	car
celular (*all*)	mobile phone/cellphone
chavo (*mex, nic, hon*)	boy
checar (*mex*)	check
chompa (*bol*)	coat

---

[14] in Spain „light bulb"!

computadora (*all*)	computer
departamento (*all*)	apartment
guagua (*arg, bol, chi, col, ecu*)	baby, child
guagua (*cub, dom, pue*)	bus
micro (*per*)	bus
jailón (*bol*)	swaggering, posh
macurcas *(bol)*	stiffness, ache
mañoso (*col, sal*)	thief
mañoso (*gua*)	lady-killer
mañoso (*per*)	depraved, corrupt
mina (*arg, bol, uru*)	woman
nomás (*all*)	only, as soon as
paja (*sal*)	silliness
pileta (*arg*)	swimming pool
pipocas (*bol*)	popcorn
plata (*arg*)	money
platicar (mex)	have a chat
relindo[15] [16] (*all*)	very nice
recontra (*all*)	utmost, highest (*+adjective*)
remera (*arg, par, uru*)	T-shirt
sonsera (*bol*)	silliness
tomar (*all*)	take (public transportation)

---

[15] „Re"+adj. is common in Latin America as an adjective intensifier. Another example is „*rebueno*" (very good).
[16] in Spain **„muy lindo"**

Exercises & games

1. Conjugate the 2nd person singular of the following verbs with "tú" or "vos":

Tú _____________ (bailar)

Vos ___________ (vivir)

Tú _____________ (sonar)

Vos ___________ (dormir)

Tú _____________ (leer)

Vos ___________ (jugar)

Tú _____________ (platicar)

Vos ___________ (checar)

2. Refer to the following words from South America with the meaning in English:

Pileta	Swimming pool
Mañoso	Silliness
Guagua	Gasoline
Carro	Take (public transportation)
Gasofa	Boy
Asado	Bus
Relindo	Woman
Mina	Depraved
Chavo	Car
Tomar	Barbecue
Paja	Very nice

Level 10
Slang

13

And we have already reached the highest level! There is probably no better way to master a language and integrate yourself than by knowing slang language terms.

Slang in Spain

¡Cierra el pico!	Shut up!
¡Es una pasada!	That's so cool!
¡Estás pirado!	You go nuts!
¡Guay!	Cool!
¡Hombre!	Wow!
¡La cagué!	It's all screwed up!
¡No te rayes!	Don't be obsessed with this!
¡Paso!	I'm not in the mood!
¡Qué fuerte!	Wicked!
¡Que te pires!	Piss off!
¡Vaya jeta!	What a cheeky bastard!
¡Vaya mierda!	What a shit!
buen rollo	good vibes, cool
chorba	girlfriend
colega	dude, buddy
coñazo	nuisance, bummer, drag
es de coña	It's a joke
estar de rechupete	to be very tasty/delicious
estar mamado	to be very drunk
estar pillado	to have a crush
finde	weekend
flipado	perplexed, freaked out
hacer pellas	to skip school
jeta	face
ligar	to flirt

Me da asco.	This really pisses me off.
molar	to be cool, to like
ni de coña	Absolutely not!
parienta	girlfriend
pavo	guy, bloke
pelota	suck-up
pibón	hot man/woman
pijo	posh
pirado	crazy
pitillo	cigarette
pringado	loser
tío	bloke, mate
tomar el pelo	to pull sb's leg
tronco	buddy, mate

Slang in Latin America

ahorita (*all*)	right now
viejos (*all*)	parents
vieja (*all*)	mother
viejo (*all*)	father
¡No mames! (*mex*)	I can't believe this!
¡Vete a la chingada! (*mex, sal*)	Go away!
chido (*mex*)	cool
chingada (*mex*)	lousy, drunk
chingón (*mex*)	excellent
cuate (*mex*)	friend, guy, buddy
culero (*mex*)	coward, cowardy custard
estar cabrón (*mex*)	to be difficult or lousy
güey (*mex*)	dude
padre (*mex*)	cool
padrísimo (*mex*)	very cool
pendejo (*mex*)	stupid
pinche (*mex*)	horrible, despicable
¿Qué onda? (*mex,arg,uru,gua,chi*)	What's up?

¿Qué pedo? (*arg*)	What's up?
boludez (*arg*)	bullshit
boludo (*arg*)	Dude!
boludo (*arg, bol, par, uru*)	fool
buena onda (*arg, chi*)	good vibes, cool
ché (*arg, uru*)	Hey!, buddy
estar al pedo (*arg*)	to have nothing to do
ni en pedo (*arg*)	no way!
orto (*arg, col, mex, per, uru*)	bum
pelotudo (*arg*)	dumbass
prenderse[17] (*arg*)	to join in a plan
quilombo (*arg*)	confusion, mess
chévere (*col,per,ven,cub,pue,ecu*)	great
estar de chaky (*bol*)	to have a hangover
ir como el orto (*chi*)	to have bad luck
joda (*arg, par, uru*)	joke
joda (*sal, mex, uru*)	pain, discomfort
irse de joda (*par, uru*)	to have a fling
la concha de la lora (*arg*)	Shit!, far away
la concha de la lora (*chi*)	far away
la concha de la lora (*cos*)	Shit!
¡No la peles! (*ecu*)	Don't bother me!
polla (*col,bol*)	bets
polla (*arg, cos, dom*)	dick
¡Qué macana! (*bol*)	Pity!
¡Pucha! (*bol, chi, per*)	Jesus!, Shit!

---

[17] in Spain „set yourself on fire"!

Exercises & games

1. Translate the following Spanish words from this level:

tío   ____________

parienta   ____________

tronco   ____________

pavo   ____________

pijo   ____________

colega   ____________

pelota   ____________

ligar   ____________

finde   ____________

pringado   ____________

molar   ____________

¡Guay!   ____________

tomar el pelo   ____________

coñazo   ____________

2. Which Latin American word would you use in the following situations?

To call a Mexican buddy   ____________________

To call a Argentinian buddy   ____________________

If you refer to the parents   ____________________

If they find something great in Mexico   ____________________

If they find something great in Peru   ____________________

If they find something great in Chile

When everything is messy in Argentina

They cannot believe their eyes in Mexico

A Paraguayan joke

When you refuse an idea in Argentina

14

You're done with the 10 levels! You can use day 14 to review the contents. Now you've become acquainted with the language and you can express yourself. Surprise the world!

Solutions

Level 1

1. 6:15 → Son las seis y cuarto.

14:00 → Son las dos (en punto).

19:50 → Son las ocho menos diez.

13:05 → Es la una y cinco.

15:35 → Son las cuatro menos veinticinco.

12:00 → Son las doce del mediodía / Es mediodía.

2. Friday, 1st March 2019 → viernes, uno de marzo de dos mil diecinueve

Friday, 8th July 2007 → viernes, ocho de julio de dos mil siete

Sunday, 4th August 1965 → domingo, cuatro de agosto de mil novecientos sesenta y cinco

Tuesday, 23rd December 1986 → martes, veintitrés de diciembre de mil novecientos ochenta y seis

3. soy, me llamo, Quién, Ella, Estás, No, com**o,** empezar**é**

Level 2

1. aeropuerto, andén, autobús, autopista, barco, bicicleta, casco, coche, gasolinera, maleta, maletero, marcha, metro, tranvía, tren

2. bicicleta, coche/carro, gasolina, tren, azafata, autobús, chófer/conductor de autobús, aire acondicionado, peaje, seguro

3. vuelo, coche, repostar, gasolinera, recogido, salida, cantimplora

Level 3

1. microondas-hotel, microondas-apartamento, microondas-cocina, camping-saco de dormir, caja fuerte-hotel, camping-prismáticos, habitación doble-hotel, habitación doble-apartamento, habitación doble-sábanas, habitación doble-mesa, habitación doble-televisor, habitación doble-calefacción, lavandería-hotel, enchufe-microondas, enchufe-tostadora, enchufe-televisor, barbacoa-camping, hotel-gimnasio, hotel-sauna, hotel-sábanas, hotel-mesa, hotel-calefacción, hotel-televisor, hotel-piscina, apartamento-cocina, apartamento-sábanas, apartamento-mesa, apartamento-calefacción, apartamento-televisor, tostadora-cocina, cocina-mesa

2. reception, room service, cama doble, ducha, bathtub, fuego, ground floor, llave de la habitación, nevera portátil, Camping gas cooker

Level 4

2. jamón, salmón, **vino**, **jerez**, jarra, plátano, bacalao, **sangría**, **paella**, solomillo, **fabada**, tortilla, cerveza, galletas, **batido**, salchichas, **espinacas**, tarta de queso, **gazpacho**, **café** con leche

Level 5

1. pintor/artista, museo, gratuita, bus turístico, zoo, Plaza, castillos, palacio, playa, montaña, frío, está lloviendo, nubes, helado, chiringuitos, castillo de arena

2.

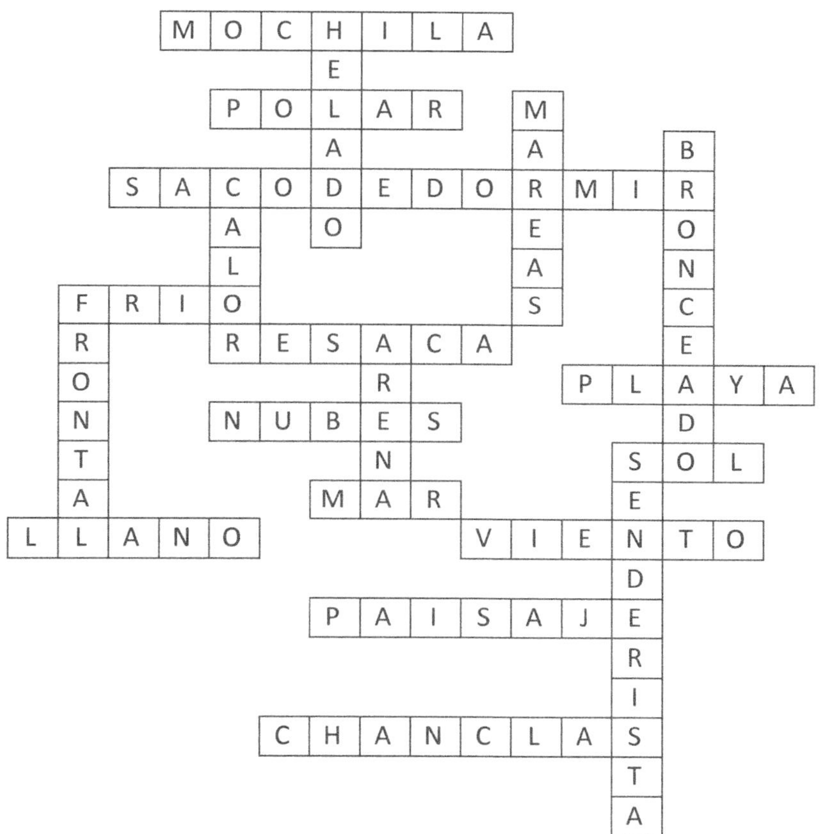

1.

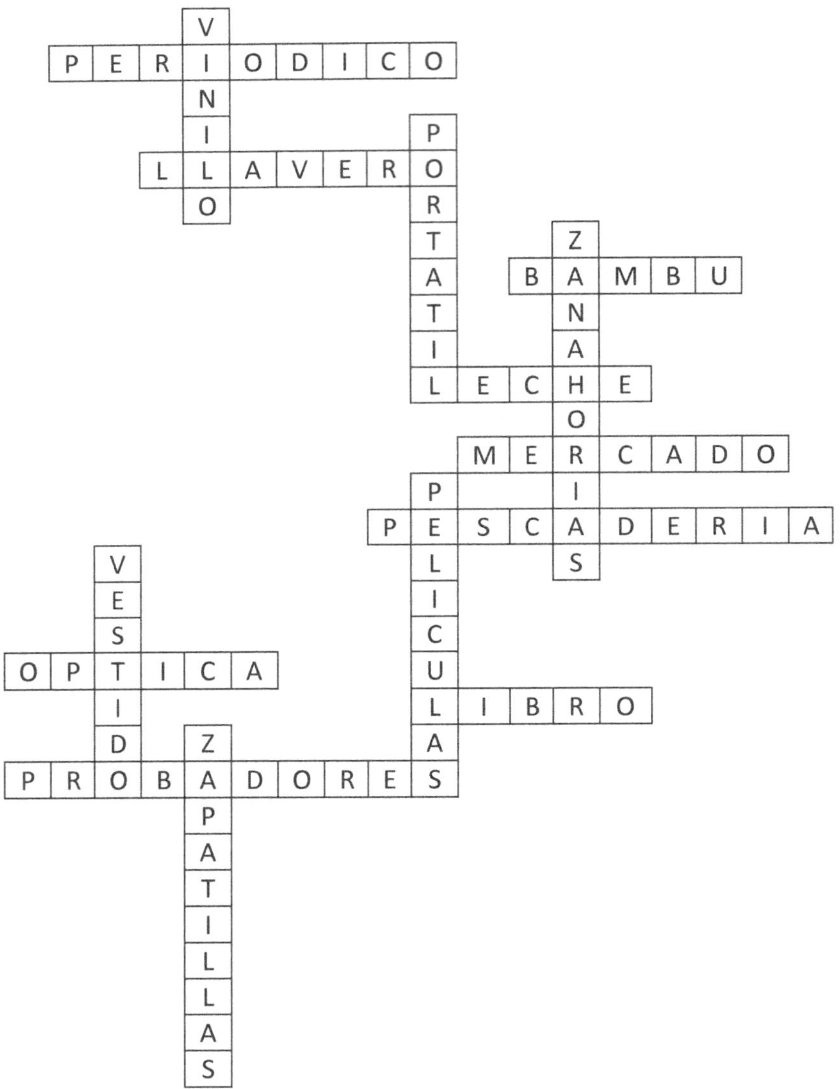

2. vino, carnicería, floristería, katiuskas, photo camera, tetería, mercadillo/rastro, diccionario, tomate, traje

Level 7

2. yoga-gimnasio, yoga-calentamiento, gimnasio-calentamiento, gimnasio-mancuernas, gimnasio-camiseta, gimnasio-abdominales, gimnasio-barra de dominadas, poste-portero, poste-larguero, torero-plaza de toros, torero-traje de luces, portero-calentamiento, portero-camiseta, portero-larguero, plaza de toros-traje de luces, tenis-calentamiento, ciclismo-calentamiento, centrocampista-calentamiento, piano-iglesia, iglesia-sacerdote, piano-canción, piano-música, piano-concierto, piano-cantante, mancuernas-barra de dominadas, cantante-música, cantante-concierto, cantante-canción, cantante-guitarrista, ciclismo-camiseta, centrocampista-camiseta, concierto-guitarrista, concierto-música, tenis-camiseta, canción-música, canción-guitarrista

Level 8

1. ¿Qué fiesta hay esta noche? *or* Qué plan hay esta noche?, Me apetece bailar salsa, ¿Dónde hay algún pub irlandés para tomar una cerveza?, ¿A qué hora quedamos esta noche?, ¿Quieres que te pase a recoger?

2. not mutual, not mutual, mutual, mutual

Level 9

1. bailas, vivís, suenas, dormís, lees, jugás, platicas, checá

2. pileta-swimming pool, mañoso-depraved, guagua-bus, carro-car, gasofa-gasoline, asado-barbecue, relindo-very nice, chavo-boy, tomar-take (public transportation), paja-silliness

Level 10

1. mate, girlfriend, buddy, guy, posh, dude, suck-up, flirt, weekend, loser, be cool *or* like, cool!, pull sb's leg, nuisance

2. güey *or* cuate, che, viejos, chido *or* padre, chévere, buena onda, quilombo, ¡No mames!, joda, ni en pedo

Bibliography

„Latin American Spanish"   lonely planet
"Fast Talk Spanish"   lonely planet
https://www.asihablamos.com/

Acknowledgments

United we stand, divided we fall. Therefore, I want to thank my sister Marta for the first cover design. Also, my friends Naira, Andrés, Luca, Pili, Mayra and Sandra, who helped me with the folk festivals, sights and vocabulary of Latin America. My thanks also to other friends who took an interest in my book even before I published it, or who cheered me on during those weeks of hard work.

And of course, I want to thank you, dear reader, for your trust. I hope that you have learned a lot, that would definitely fulfill me and motivate me even more. If you liked my book, I'd appreciate you spending a couple of minutes sending your review to support@pld-publishing.com, just like other engaged readers. That will surely help to become better and provide the best service to readers like you

I am glad to reveal this gift for you: Spanish flashcards via Anki. Anki is a powerful learning app that simplifies language learning. Our custom flashcard catalogue aligns with your book's lessons, featuring audio for pronunciation, visuals to aid memory, and spaced repetition to ensure lasting retention.

https://tinyurl.com/learn-Spanish-pld

Follow me on Facebook, Instagram, TikTok, or YouTube for free resources to level up your Spanish!

IG:	@leobabel_pld
TikTok:	@leobabel_spa
YouTube:	youtube.pld-publishing.de
Facebook:	https://www.facebook.com/leobabel.books

And if you are serious about taking your Spanish to the next level, you can apply for a place in my Spanish coaching, aimed at working with you personally to reach your goals. You can fill in this form so that I get to know your situation: https://forms.gle/H6y2pVjJc9W52Xvg7

Legal

Image attributions

Cover

Main element (amended)
Depositphotos, ID vector: 59687951, Copyright: 3dsparrow

Background (Spanish flag)
shutterstock

Logo

Mug and book
Vector de Café creado por freepik - www.freepik.es

Book
Vector de Fondo creado por freepik - www.freepik.es

Other images in the book

Spanish map on Page 10
Image by Maria_Alberto from Pixabay

Latin American map on Page 17
https://commons.wikimedia.org/wiki/File:Voseo-extension-real.PNG (Lizenz *Creative Commons Attribution-Share Alike 3.0 Unported*, verändert)

Photo Beach
Photo by Jorge Fernández Salas on Unsplash

Photo Hiking
Photo by Austin Fruits on Unsplash

Icon Shopping bag
Icons made by Smashicons from www.flaticon.com

Icon Paella
Icons made by Eucalyp from www.flaticon.com

Icons plate and cutlery, airplane, bus, bicycle, traveler carrying suitcase, staircase, parasol and sun, hotel, Thank you icon, conversation, envelope, shopping cart, calendar, South America map, audio CD, light bulb, tent, bowling, soccer, guitar, skyline, playing cards, airport, fast forward, clock, book, train, thermometer, taxi, pizza, car, beer, mate, carnival mask, anchor, cookies, cup of coffee and hiker
Icons made by Freepik from www.flaticon.com

Icon dumbbell
Icons made by Elias Bikbulatov from www.flaticon.com